Geology

Geology

Edited by Barbara A. Woyt

Britannica Educational Publishing

IN ASSOCIATION WITH

ROSEN EDUCATIONAL SERVICES

Published in 2017 by Britannica Educational Publishing (a trademark of Encyclopædia Britannica, Inc.) in association with The Rosen Publishing Group, Inc.
29 East 21st Street, New York, NY 10010

Distributed exclusively by Rosen Publishing.
To see additional Britannica Educational Publishing titles, go to rosenpublishing.com.

First Edition

Britannica Educational Publishing
J.E. Luebering: Executive Director, Core Editorial
Anthony L. Green: Editor, Compton's by Britannica

Rosen Publishing
Kathy Kuhtz Campbell: Senior Editor
Nelson Sá: Art Director
Brian Garvey: Designer
Cindy Reiman: Photography Manager
Bruce Donnola: Photo Researcher
Supplementary text by Barbara A. Woyt

Library of Congress Cataloging-in-Publication Data

Names: Woyt, Barbara A., editor.
Title: Geology / edited by Barbara A. Woyt.
Other titles: Study of science.
Description: First edition. | New York : Britannica Educational Publishing in Association with Rosen Educational Services, 2017. | Series: The study of science | Audience: Grades 7 to 12. | Includes bibliographical references and index.
Identifiers: LCCN 2016024164 | ISBN 9781508104261 (library bound)
Subjects: LCSH: Geology--Juvenile literature. | Earth sciences--Juvenile literature. | Earth (Planet)--Juvenile literature.
Classification: LCC QE29 .G46 2017 | DDC 550--dc23
LC record available at https://lccn.loc.gov/2016024164

Manufactured in China

Photo credits: Cover, p. 3 Marco Restivo/Moment/Getty Images; pp. 8-9 Hawaii Volcano Observatory/U.S. Geological Survey; p. 14 MarcelClemens/Shutterstock.com; pp. 18, 42, 51, 61, 67, 85 Encyclopædia Britannica, Inc.; p. 20 © Len Collection/Alamy Stock Photo; p. 24 Science Stock Photography/Science Source; p. 39 AFP/Getty Images; p. 53 Pacific Press/LightRocket/Getty Images; p. 58 Ken M. Johns/Science Source; p. 65 © Ulrich Doering/Alamy Stock Photo; p. 73 Jeff Topping/Getty Images; p. 76 Education Images/Universal Images Group/Getty Images; p. 78 Frank Bienewald/LightRocket/Getty Images; p. 80 Universal Images Group/Getty Images; p. 82 © Ron Niebrugge/Alamy Stock; p. 89 Lyn Alweis/The Denver Post/Getty Images; p. 94 Aizar Raldes/AFP/Getty Images; p. 97 © Marvin Dembinsky Photo Associates/Alamy Stock Photo; p. 100 Time Life Pictures/The LIFE Picture Collection/Getty Images; p. 105 © AP Images; p. 107 © Greenshoots Communications/Alamy Stock Photo; p. 110 Ana Fernandez/AFP/Getty Images; p. 112 AGF/Universal Images Group/Getty Images; p. 114 Universal History Archive/Universal Images Group/Getty Images; p. 118 The Washington Post/Getty Images; p. 122 Jon Wilson/Science Source; cover and interior pages backgrounds and borders © iStockphoto.com/LuMaxArt.

CONTENTS

INTRODUCTION

A geologist uses a rock hammer to sample active pahoehoe lava for geochemical analysis on the Kilauea volcano, Hawaii. Pahoehoe is a Hawaiian name for a type of cooled, hard lava that has a smooth, often billowy shiny surface.

The earth sciences seek to understand the features and phenomena of Earth, its waters, and its atmosphere. In general, the earth sciences focus on the present features and the past evolution of Earth. This includes the many physical and chemical—and some biological—aspects of Earth's atmosphere, waters, surface, and internal structure.

Perhaps the broadest of the earth sciences is geology, the study of the history, structure, and composition of the solid Earth, and of the past and present processes that act on it. Geology encompasses sciences such as mineralogy (the study of minerals) and stratigraphy (the study of rock layers), and includes a wealth of sub- and cross-disciplines, including geophysics and geochemistry.

An introduction to the geological sciences logically begins with mineralogy, because Earth's rocks are composed of minerals. A principal concern of mineralogy is the chemical analysis of the some 3,000 known minerals that are the chief constituents of

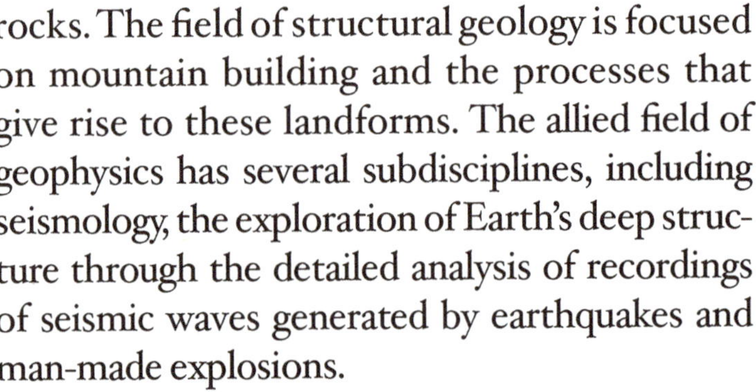

rocks. The field of structural geology is focused on mountain building and the processes that give rise to these landforms. The allied field of geophysics has several subdisciplines, including seismology, the exploration of Earth's deep structure through the detailed analysis of recordings of seismic waves generated by earthquakes and man-made explosions.

Geomorphology is concerned with the surface processes of weathering and erosion that create the landscapes of the world. Knowledge of these processes is important for understanding not only the development of landscapes but also the ways in which sediments are created.

Geologic history provides a conceptual framework and overview of the evolution of the Earth. An early development of the subject was stratigraphy, the study of order and sequence in bedded sedimentary rocks. Today biostratigraphy uses fossils to characterize successive intervals of geologic time. The geologic time scale, back to the oldest rocks some 4.28 billion years ago, can be quantified by isotopic dating techniques. This is the science of geochronology. Paleontology, the study of fossils, is concerned not only with their description and classification but also with an analysis of the evolution of the organisms involved.

Several disciplines of the geologic sciences have practical benefits for society. The geologist is responsible for the discovery of minerals, which are the main economic resources of Earth; for the application of knowledge of subsurface structures and geologic conditions to the building industry; and for the prevention of natural hazards or at least providing early warning of their occurrence.

Astrogeology is important in that it contributes to understanding the development of Earth within the solar system. The US Apollo program of manned missions to the Moon, for example, provided scientists with firsthand information on lunar geology, including observations on such features as meteorite craters that are relatively rare on Earth. Unmanned space probes have yielded significant data on the surface features of many of the planets and their satellites.

Readers of this resource will examine many of the subdisciplines of geology and reflect on their significant contributions to our understanding of the solid Earth and the structure of its interior.

Chapter 1

The Study of Earth's Composition

The fields of geology that focus on Earth's composition are considered in this chapter. Among the most fundamental of these is the science of mineralogy, which deals with minerals in the Earth's crust and those found outside the Earth, such as lunar samples and meteorites. Mineralogists study the formation, occurrence, chemical and physical properties, composition, and classification of minerals, as well as the external form and internal structure of natural and synthetic crystals.

Petrology deals with the origin, occurrence, structure, and history of rocks, especially igneous and metamorphic rocks. Petrologists study changes that occur in rock masses when magmas solidify, when solid rocks melt partially or wholly, and when sediments undergo chemical or physical transformation.

Economic geology, which is sometimes called geological engineering, links mining and civil engineering. It involves the application of geological principles to the study of soil, rock materials, and groundwater as they affect the planning, design, location, construction, operation, and maintenance of engineering structures. Economic geologists study the distribution of mineral deposits, the economic considerations involved in their recovery, and assessments of the reserves that are available.

Geochemistry is concerned with the chemistry of Earth as a whole. Geochemists are interested in the origin and evolution of the major classes of rocks and minerals, and they specifically study the distribution and amounts of the chemical elements in minerals, rocks, soils, life forms, water, and the atmosphere.

MINERALOGY

As a discipline, mineralogy has close historical ties with geology. Minerals, as the basic constituents of rocks and ore deposits, are an integral aspect of geology. The problems and techniques of mineralogy, however, are distinct in many respects from those of the rest of geology, with the result that mineralogy has grown to be a large, complex discipline in itself.

About 3,000 distinct mineral species are recognized, but relatively few are important

Samples of rocks and minerals are pictured here, including fluorite on quartz (*fourth row, third from left*); chalcanthite (*third row, fourth from left*), which is a copper mineral; and amazonite (*third row, first mineral from left*), which is a type of feldspar.

in the kinds of rocks that are abundant in the outer part of Earth. Thus a few minerals such as the feldspars, quartz, and mica are the essential ingredients in granite and closely related rocks.

Limestones, which are widely distributed on all continents, consist largely of only two minerals, calcite and dolomite. Many rocks have a more complex mineralogy; in some the mineral particles are so minute that they can be identified only through specialized techniques.

It is possible to identify an individual mineral in a specimen by examining and testing its physical properties. Determining the hardness of a mineral is the most practical way of identifying it. This can be done by using the Mohs scale of hardness, which lists 10 common minerals in their relative order of hardness: talc (softest with the scale number 1), gypsum (2), calcite (3), fluorite (4), apatite (5), orthoclase (6), quartz (7), topaz (8), corundum (9), and diamond (10). Harder minerals scratch softer ones, so that an unknown mineral can be readily positioned between minerals on the scale. Certain common objects that have been assigned hardness values roughly corresponding to those of the Mohs scale (for example, a fingernail [2.5], pocketknife blade [5.5], and steel file [6.5]) are usually used in conjunction with the minerals on the scale for additional reference.

Other physical properties of minerals that aid in identification are crystal form, cleavage type, fracture, streak, luster, color, specific gravity, and density. In addition, the refractive

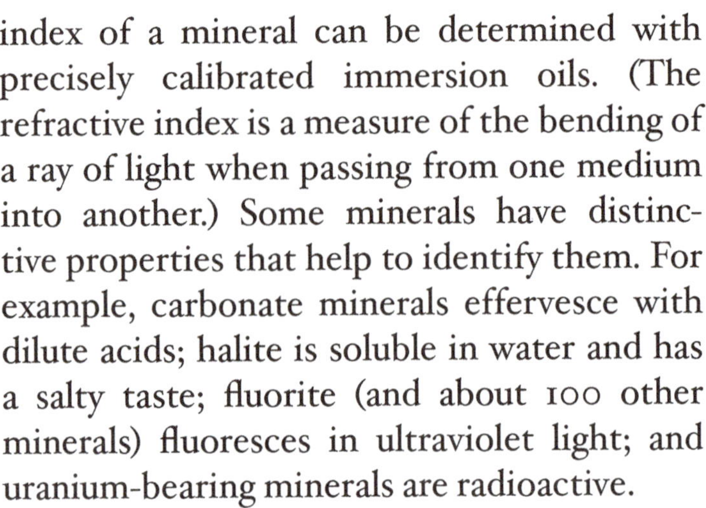

index of a mineral can be determined with precisely calibrated immersion oils. (The refractive index is a measure of the bending of a ray of light when passing from one medium into another.) Some minerals have distinctive properties that help to identify them. For example, carbonate minerals effervesce with dilute acids; halite is soluble in water and has a salty taste; fluorite (and about 100 other minerals) fluoresces in ultraviolet light; and uranium-bearing minerals are radioactive.

The science of crystallography is concerned with the geometric properties and internal structure of crystals. Because minerals are generally crystalline, crystallography is an essential aspect of mineralogy. Investigators in the field may use a reflecting goniometer that measures angles between crystal faces to help determine the crystal system to which a mineral belongs. Another important instrument that they frequently employ is the X-ray diffractometer, which makes use of the fact that X-rays, when passing through a mineral specimen, are diffracted at regular angles. The paths of the diffracted rays are recorded on photographic film, and the positions and intensities of the resulting diffraction lines on the film provide a particular pattern. Every mineral has its own unique diffraction pattern,

CRYSTALS

The ancient Greeks used the word *krystallos* to mean both ice and quartz. They thought that quartz was simply another form of ice that had become permanently solid. Today a crystal is commonly considered to be a solid object with symmetrically arranged flat surfaces that meet in straight lines and sharp corners. Everyone has seen examples of such crystals. Diamonds, snowflakes, and rock salt are among the best known.

The scientific definition of a crystal is based on its internal structure rather than its outward appearance. All matter on Earth is made up of atoms or, more frequently, combinations of atoms called molecules. If the molecules of a substance are arranged in a regular repeating pattern, the substance is a crystal. The segment of the pattern that is repeated over and over is called the unit cell. The three-dimensional pattern, made up of many unit cells lined up in all directions, is called the crystal lattice. The form of the crystal depends on the arrangement of the molecules within it. For example, the molecules of sodium chloride (table salt) are arranged in a cubic pattern. As a result, sodium chloride crystals are cubic in appearance.

Most solids are composed of crystals. Nearly all metals and many other minerals are crystalline solids. On the other hand, glass, most plastics, and rubber belong to a different class of solids. These noncrystalline, or amorphous, solids have a less orderly arrangement of their molecules. Many substances, including rocks, dirt, and concrete, are mixtures of different kinds of solids. Various organic materials—wood, wheat, and wool, for example—are complex mixtures, containing long chains of molecules. Simpler

(continued on the next page)

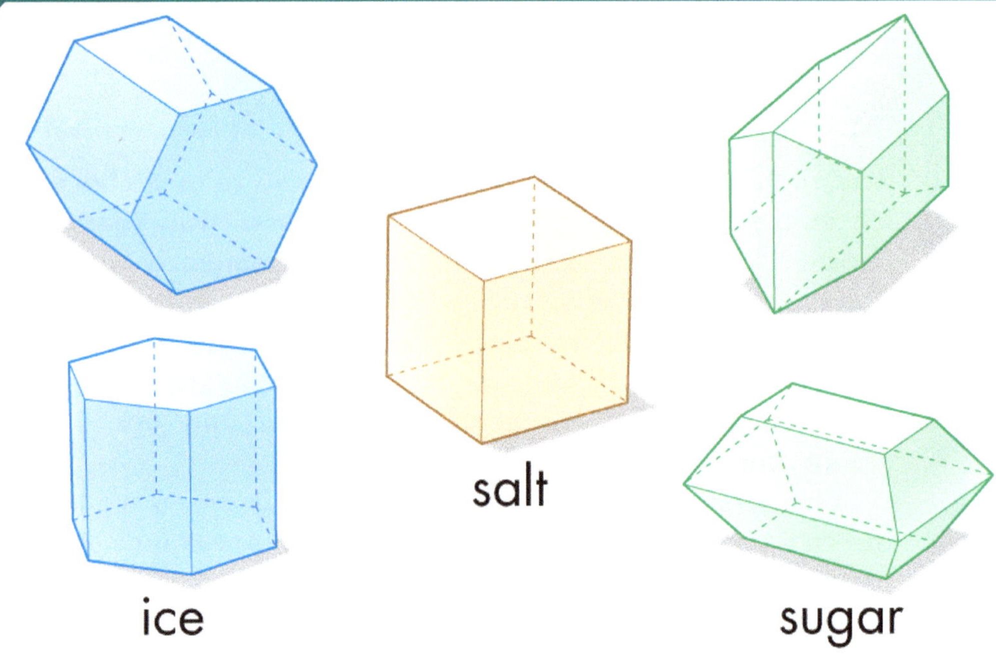

Different substances form different crystal shapes, as is shown in this example of ice, salt, and sugar. But all crystals of the same substance have the same shape.

(continued from the previous page)

organic compounds, and even some viruses, are often crystalline in structure.

Liquid crystals are not actually crystals but rather are substances with some properties of liquids and some of crystalline solids. They can flow like liquids but also display some of the ordered structure of a crystal.

Some solid materials, such as metals, salts, and powders, do not fit the common notion of crystals but do fit the scientific definition. The solids that fit the common notion of crystals are all large single crystals. In a single crystal the same orientation of the crystal pattern extends throughout the specimen. When this occurs, the

symmetrical arrangement of the unit cells can show up in the overall appearance of the crystal.

Most common solids are polycrystalline, composed of many crystals. Their molecules are arranged in a pattern, but a given orientation of the pattern extends over only a small area, called a grain. Each grain shows the symmetry that is observed in large single crystals.

so crystallographers are able to determine not only the crystal structure of a mineral but the type of mineral as well.

When a complex substance such as a magma crystallizes to form igneous rock, the grains of different constituent minerals grow together and mutually interfere, with the result that they do not retain their externally recognizable crystal form. To study the minerals in such a rock, the mineralogist uses a petrographic microscope constructed for viewing thin sections of the rock, which are ground uniformly to a thickness of about 0.03 millimeter, in light polarized by two polarizing prisms in the microscope. If the rock is crystalline, its essential minerals can be determined by their peculiar optical properties as revealed in transmitted light under magnification, provided that the individual crystal grains can be distinguished.

A researcher uses an electron probe microanalyzer to examine the elemental composition of samples of copper indium gallium diselenide, or CIGS, often used in semiconductor materials.

Opaque minerals, such as those with a high content of metallic elements, require a technique employing reflected light from polished surfaces. This kind of microscopic analysis has particular application to metallic ore minerals. The polarizing microscope, however, has a lower limit to the size of grains that can be distinguished with the eye; even the best microscopes cannot resolve grains less than about 0.5 micrometer (0.0005 millimeter) in diameter. For higher magnifications the mineralogist uses an electron microscope, which produces images with diameters enlarged tens of thousands of times.

The methods just described pertain to the study of the physical properties of minerals. Another important area of mineralogy concerns the chemical composition of minerals. The primary instrument used is the electron microprobe. Here a beam of electrons is focused on a thin section of rock that has been highly polished and coated with carbon. The electron beam can be narrowed to a diameter of about one micrometer and thus can be focused on a single grain of a mineral, which can be observed with an ordinary optical microscope system. The electrons cause the atoms in the mineral under examination to emit diagnostic X-rays, the intensity and concentration of

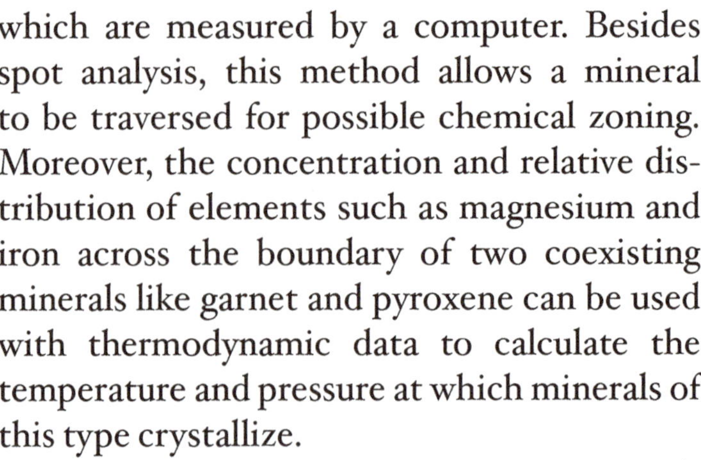

which are measured by a computer. Besides spot analysis, this method allows a mineral to be traversed for possible chemical zoning. Moreover, the concentration and relative distribution of elements such as magnesium and iron across the boundary of two coexisting minerals like garnet and pyroxene can be used with thermodynamic data to calculate the temperature and pressure at which minerals of this type crystallize.

Although the major concern of mineralogy is to describe and classify the properties of minerals, it is also concerned with their origin. Physical chemistry and thermodynamics are basic tools for understanding mineral origin. Some observational data are concerned with the behavior of solutions in precipitating crystalline materials under controlled conditions in the laboratory. Certain minerals can be created synthetically under conditions in which temperature and concentration of solutions are carefully monitored. Other experimental methods include study of the transformation of solids at high temperatures and pressures to yield specific minerals or assemblages of minerals. Experimental data obtained in the laboratory, coupled with chemical and physical theory, enable the conditions of origin of many naturally occurring minerals to be inferred.

PETROLOGY

Petrology is the study of rocks. Because most rocks are composed of minerals, petrology is strongly dependent on mineralogy. In many respects mineralogy and petrology share the same problems; for example, the physical conditions that prevail (pressure, temperature, time, and presence or absence of water) when particular minerals or mineral assemblages are formed. Although petrology is in principle concerned with rocks throughout the crust, as well as with those far below Earth's surface, in practice the discipline deals mainly with those that are accessible in the outer part of the crust. Rock specimens obtained from the surface of the Moon and from other planets are also considerations of petrology. Fields of specialization in petrology correspond to the three major rock types—igneous, sedimentary, and metamorphic.

IGNEOUS PETROLOGY

Igneous petrology is concerned with the identification, classification, origin, evolution, and processes of formation and

Examples of igneous rocks include (*clockwise, top left*) obsidian, gabbro, granite porphyry, pumice, and andesite. Igneous petrology deals with the origin, history, occurrence, structure, chemical makeup, and classification of igneous rocks.

crystallization of igneous rocks (rocks formed by the cooling and solidification of magma, a molten or partially molten rocky material). Most of the rocks available for study come from Earth's crust, but a few, such as eclogites, derive from the mantle.

The scope of igneous petrology is very large because igneous rocks make up the bulk of the continental and oceanic crusts and of the mountain belts of the world; they also include high-level volcanic extrusive rocks and igneous rocks that formed deep within the crust.

Of utmost importance to igneous petrologic research is geochemistry, which is concerned with the major- and trace-element composition of igneous rocks as well as of the magmas from which they arose. Some of the major problems within the scope of igneous petrology are: the form and structure of igneous bodies, and their relations to surrounding rocks; the crystallization history of the minerals that make up igneous rocks (this is determined with the petrographic polarizing microscope); the classification of rocks based on textural features, grain size, and the abundance and composition of constituent minerals; various studies of the parent magmas from which igneous rocks form; the history of formation and the composition of oceanic crust; the evolution of igneous rocks through geologic time; the composition of the mantle; and the conditions of pressure and temperature at which different magmas form and at which their igneous products crystallize (determined from high-pressure experimental petrology).

The basic instrument of igneous petrology is the petrographic polarizing microscope, but the majority of instruments used today have to do with determining rock and mineral chemistry. These include the X-ray fluorescence spectrometer, equipment for neutron activation

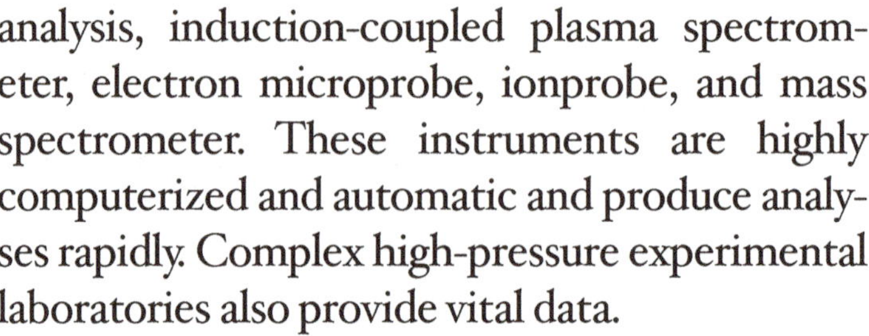

analysis, induction-coupled plasma spectrometer, electron microprobe, ionprobe, and mass spectrometer. These instruments are highly computerized and automatic and produce analyses rapidly. Complex high-pressure experimental laboratories also provide vital data.

With a vast array of sophisticated instruments available, the igneous petrologist is able to answer many fundamental questions. Study of the ocean floor has been combined with investigation of ophiolite complexes, slices of the ocean floor that have been thrust above sea level by the action of plate tectonics. A combination of mineral chemistry and experimental petrology allows investigators to calculate the depth and temperature of the magma chambers situated along mid-ocean ridges. The depths are close to four miles (six kilometers), and the temperatures range from 2,102 °F to 2,334 °F (1,150 °C to 1,279 °C).

In 1974 geologists B.W. Chappell and A.J.R. White discovered two major and distinct types of granitic rock—namely, I- and S-type granitoids. Analysis of the chemical ratios of two strontium isotopes, as well as mineral content indicated the I-type rocks formed above subduction zones in island arcs and active (subducting) continental margins and were ultimately derived by partial melting of mantle and subducted oceanic lithosphere. In contrast, S-type granitoids were formed by partial melting of lower continental crust. Those found in the Himalayas were formed during the Miocene Epoch some 20,000,000 years ago as a result of the penetration of India into Asia, which thickened the continental crust and then caused its partial melting.

In the island arcs and active continental margins that rim the Pacific Ocean, there are many different volcanic and plutonic rocks (igneous rocks formed from magma slowly cooling below Earth's surface) belonging to the calc-alkaline series. (A rock series is an assemblage of rock types that share certain characters; rocks of the calc-alkaline series are rich in alkali metals and alkaline earths, especially calcium oxide.) These include basalt; andesite; dacite; rhyolite; ignimbrite; diorite; granite; peridotite; gabbro; and tonalite, trondhjemite, and granodiorite (TTG). They occur typically in vast batholiths, which may reach several thousand kilometers in length and contain more than 1,000 separate granitic bodies. These TTG calc-alkaline rocks represent the main means of growth of the continental crust throughout geologic time. Much research is devoted to them in an effort to determine the source regions of their parent magmas and the chemical evolution of the magmas.

SEDIMENTARY PETROLOGY

The field of sedimentary petrology is concerned with the description and classification of sedimentary rocks, interpretation of the processes of transportation and deposition of the sedimentary materials forming the rocks, the environment that prevailed at the time the sediments were deposited, and the alteration (compaction, cementation, and chemical and mineralogical modification) of the sediments after deposition.

There are two main branches of sedimentary petrology. One branch deals with carbonate rocks, namely limestones and dolomites, composed principally of calcium carbonate (calcite) and calcium magnesium carbonate (dolomite). Much of the complexity in classifying carbonate rocks stems partly from the fact that many limestones and dolomites have been formed, directly or indirectly, through the influence of organisms, including bacteria, lime-secreting algae, various shelled organisms (for example, mollusks and brachiopods), and by corals. In limestones and dolomites that were deposited under marine conditions, commonly in shallow warm seas, much of the material initially forming the rock consists of skeletons of lime-secreting organisms. In many examples, this skeletal material is preserved as fossils. Some of the major problems of carbonate petrology concern the physical and biological conditions of the environments in which carbonate material has been deposited, including water depth, temperature, degree of illumination by sunlight, motion by waves and currents, and the salinity and other chemical aspects of the water in which deposition occurred.

The other principal branch of sedimentary petrology is concerned with the sediments and sedimentary rocks that are essentially noncalcareous. These include sands and sandstones, clays and claystones, siltstones, conglomerates, glacial till, and varieties of sandstones, siltstones, and conglomerates (such as the graywacke-type sandstones and siltstones). These rocks are broadly known as clastic rocks because they consist of distinct particles or clasts. Clastic petrology is concerned with classification, particularly with respect to the mineral composition of fragments or particles, as well as the shapes of particles (angular versus rounded), and the degree of homogeneity of particle sizes. Other main concerns of clastic petrology are the mode of transportation of sedimentary materials, including the transportation of clay, silt, and fine sand by wind; and the transportation of

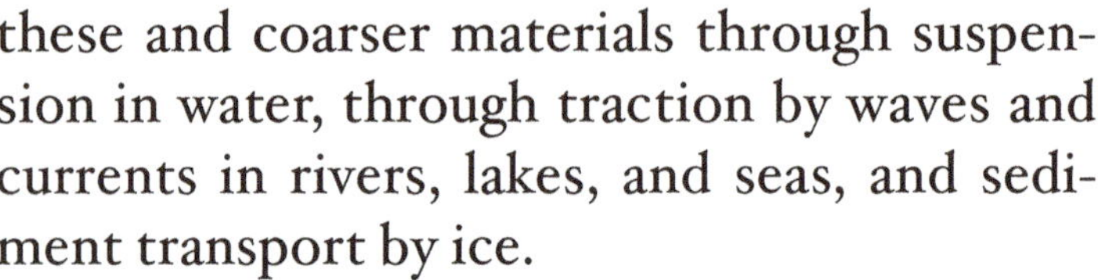

these and coarser materials through suspension in water, through traction by waves and currents in rivers, lakes, and seas, and sediment transport by ice.

Sedimentary petrology also is concerned with the small-scale structural features of sediments and sedimentary rocks. Features that can be conveniently seen in a specimen held in the hand are within the domain of sedimentary petrology. These features include the geometrical attitude of mineral grains with respect to each other, small-scale cross stratification, the shapes and interconnections of pore spaces, and the presence of fractures and veinlets.

Instruments and methods used by sedimentary petrologists include the petrographic microscope for description and classification, X-ray mineralogy for defining fabrics and small-scale structures, physical model flume experiments for studying the effects of flow as an agent of transport and the development of sedimentary structures, and mass spectrometry for calculating stable isotopes and the temperatures of deposition, cementation, and diagenesis. Wet-suit diving permits direct observation of current processes on coral reefs, and manned submersibles enable observation at depth on the ocean floor and in mid-oceanic ridges.

The theory of plate tectonics has given rise to much interest in the relationships between sedimentation and tectonics, particularly in modern plate-tectonic environments—for example, spreading-related settings (intracontinental rifts, early stages of intercontinental rifting such as the Red Sea, and late stages of intercontinental rifting such as the margins of the present Atlantic Ocean), mid-oceanic settings (ridges and transform faults), subduction-related settings (volcanic arcs, fore-arcs, back-arcs, and trenches), and continental collision-related settings (the Alpine-Himalayan belt, among others). Today many subdisciplines of sedimentary petrology are concerned with the detailed investigation of the various sedimentary processes that occur within these plate-tectonic environments.

METAMORPHIC PETROLOGY

Metamorphism means change in form. In geology the term is used to refer to a solid-state recrystallization of earlier igneous, sedimentary, or metamorphic rocks. There are two main types of metamorphism: (1) contact metamorphism, in which changes induced largely by increase in temperature are localized at the contacts of igneous intrusions; and (2) regional

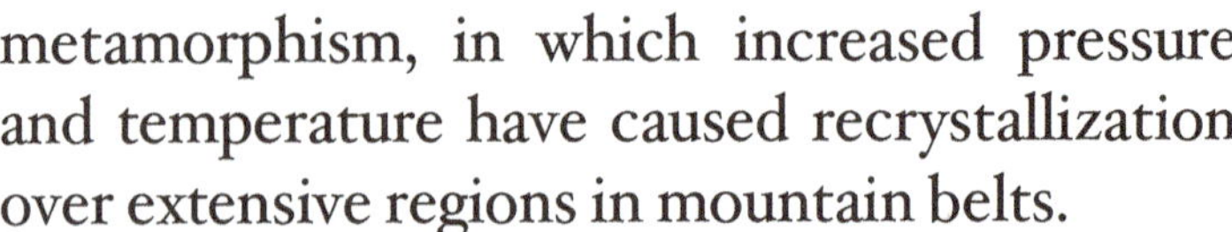

metamorphism, in which increased pressure and temperature have caused recrystallization over extensive regions in mountain belts.

Metamorphic petrology is concerned with field relations and local tectonic environments; the description and classification of the texture and chemistry of metamorphic rocks; the study of minerals and their chemistry, which yields data on the temperatures and pressures at which the rocks recrystallized; and the study of conditions and structures that provide information about the tectonic conditions under which regional metamorphic rocks formed.

A supplement to metamorphism is metasomatism: the introduction and expulsion of fluids and elements through rocks during recrystallization. When new crust is formed and metamorphosed at a mid-oceanic ridge, seawater penetrates into the crust for a few kilometers and carries a large amount of sodium with it. During formation of a contact metamorphic aureole around a granitic intrusion, hydrothermal fluids carrying elements such as iron, boron, and fluorine pass from the granite into the wall rocks. When the continental crust is thickened, its lower part may suffer dehydration and form granulites. The expelled fluids, carrying such heat-producing elements as rubidium, uranium, and thorium migrate upward into the upper crust. Much petrologic research is concerned with determining the amount and composition of fluids that have passed through rocks during these metamorphic processes.

The basic instrument used by the metamorphic petrologist is the petrographic microscope, which allows detailed study and definition of mineral types, assemblages, and reactions. If a heating/freezing stage is attached to the microscope, the temperature of formation and composition of fluid inclusions within minerals can be calculated. The electron microprobe is widely used for analyzing the composition of the component minerals. The petrologist can combine the mineral chemistry with data from experimental studies and thermodynamics to calculate the pressures and temperatures at which the rocks recrystallized. By obtaining information on the isotopic age of successive metamorphic events with a mass spectrometer, pressure–temperature–time curves can be worked out. These curves chart the movement of the rocks over time as they were brought to the surface from deep within the continental crust; this technique is important for understanding metamorphic processes. Some continental metamorphic rocks that contain diamonds and coesites (ultrahigh pressure minerals) have been carried down subduction zones to a depth of at least 60 miles (100 kilometers), brought up, and often exposed at the present surface within collisional orogenic belts, such as the Swiss Alps, the Himalayas, the Kokchetav metamorphic terrane in Kazakhstan, and the Variscan belt in Germany. These examples demonstrate that metamorphic petrology plays a key role in unraveling tectonic processes in mountain belts that have passed through the plate-tectonic cycle of events.

ECONOMIC GEOLOGY

The mineral commodities on which modern civilization is heavily dependent are obtained from Earth's crust and have a prominent place in the study and practice of economic geology. In turn, economic geology consists of several principal branches that include the study of ore deposits, petroleum geology, and the geology of nonmetallic deposits (excluding petroleum), such as coal, stone, salt, gypsum, clay and sand, and other commercially valuable materials.

The practice of economic geology is distinguished by the fact that its objectives are to aid in the exploration for and extraction of mineral resources. The objectives are therefore economic. In petroleum geology, for example, a common goal is to guide oil-well drilling programs so that the most profitable prospects are drilled and those that are likely to be of marginal economic value, or barren, are avoided. A similar philosophy influences the other branches of economic geology. In this sense, economic geology can be considered an aspect of business that is devoted to economic decision making. Many deposits of economic interest, particularly those of metallic ores, are of extreme scientific interest in themselves, however, and they have warranted intensive study that has been somewhat apart from economic considerations.

The practice of economic geology provides employment for a large number of geologists. On a worldwide basis, probably more than two-thirds of those persons employed in the geologic sciences are engaged in work that touches on the economic aspects of geology. These include geologists whose main interests lie in diverse fields of the geologic sciences. For example, the petroleum industry, which collectively is the largest employer of economic geologists, attracts individuals with specialties in stratigraphy, sedimentary petrology, structural geology, paleontology, and geophysics.

GEOCHEMISTRY

The subdiscipline of geology deals with the relative abundance, distribution, and migration of the Earth's chemical elements and their isotopes.

EARTH'S CHEMISTRY

Geochemistry is broadly concerned with the application of chemistry to virtually all aspects of geology. Inasmuch as the Earth is composed of chemical elements, all geologic materials and most geologic processes can be regarded from a chemical point of view. Some of the major problems that broadly belong to geochemistry include the origin and abundance of the elements in the solar system, galaxy, and universe (cosmochemistry); the abundance of elements in the major divisions of the Earth, including the core, mantle, crust, hydrosphere, and atmosphere; the behavior of ions in the structure of crystals; the chemical reactions in cooling magmas and the origin and evolution of deeply buried intrusive igneous rocks; the chemistry of volcanic (extrusive) igneous rocks and of phenomena closely related to volcanic activity, including hot-spring activity, emanation of volcanic gases, and origin of ore deposits formed by hot waters derived during the late stages of cooling of igneous magmas; chemical reactions involved in weathering of rocks in which earlier formed minerals decay and new minerals are created; the transportation of weathering products in solution by natural waters in the ground and in streams, lakes, and the sea; chemical changes that accompany formation of sedimentary rocks; and the progressive chemical and mineralogical changes that take place as rocks undergo metamorphism.

One of the leading general concerns of geochemistry is the continual recycling of the materials of the Earth. This process takes place in several ways: (1) It is widely believed that oceanic and continental basalts crystallized from magmas that were ultimately derived by the partial melting of Earth's mantle. Much geochemical research is devoted to quantifying this extraction of mantle material and its contribution to crustal growth throughout geologic time in seafloor formation and mountain building. (2) When the basalts that formed at the mid-oceanic ridge are transported across the ocean by the process of seafloor spreading, they interact with seawater, adding sodium to the basaltic crust and extracting calcium from it. (3) Geophysical data confirm the idea that the oceanic lithosphere is being consumed along Earth's major subduction zones below the continental lithosphere—for example, along the continental margin of the Andes Mountain Ranges. Many geochemists are studying what happens to this subducted material and how it contributes to the growth of island arcs and Andean-type mountain belts. (4) The behavior of dissolved materials in natural waters, under the relatively low temperatures that prevail at or near the surface of the Earth, is an integral aspect of the crustal cycle. Weathering processes supply dissolved material, including silica, calcium carbonate, and other salts, to streams. These materials then enter the oceans, where some remain in solution, whereas others are progressively removed to form certain sedimentary rocks and mineral deposits.

The behavior of biological materials and their subsequent disposition are important aspects of geochemistry, generally termed organic geochemistry and biogeochemistry. Major problems of organic geochemistry include the question of the chemical environment on Earth in which life originated; the modification of the hydrosphere and the atmosphere through the effects of life; and the incorporation of organic materials in rocks, including carbonaceous material in sedimentary rocks. The nature and chemical transformations of biological material present in deposits of coal, petroleum, and natural gas lie within the scope of organic geochemistry. Organic chemical reactions influence many geochemical processes, as, for example, rock weathering and production of soil, the solution,

In 2004 the Mars exploration rover *Spirit* reached out with its robot arm to photograph with a microscopic lens Martian soil for the first time. Geochemistry includes the study of the rocks, soils, and elements of other planets.

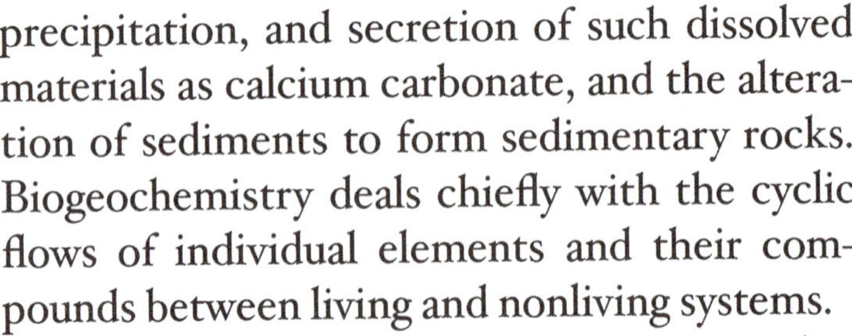

precipitation, and secretion of such dissolved materials as calcium carbonate, and the alteration of sediments to form sedimentary rocks. Biogeochemistry deals chiefly with the cyclic flows of individual elements and their compounds between living and nonliving systems.

Geochemistry has applications to other subdisciplines within geology, as well as to disciplines relatively far removed from it. At one extreme, geochemistry is linked with cosmology in a number of ways. These include the study of the chemical composition of meteorites, the relative abundance of elements in Earth, the Moon, and other planets, and the ages of meteorites and of rocks of the crust of Earth and the Moon as established by radiometric means. At the other extreme, the geochemistry of traces of metals in rocks and soils and, ultimately, in the food chain has important consequences for humans and for the vast body of lesser organisms on which they are dependent and with whom they coexist. Deficiencies in traces of copper and cobalt in forage plants, for example, lead to diseases in certain grazing animals and may locally influence human health. These deficiencies are in turn related to the concentrations of these elements in rocks and the manner in which they are chemically combined within soils and rocks.

The chemical analysis of minerals is undertaken with the electron microprobe. Instruments and techniques used for the chemical analysis of rocks includes the X-ray fluorescent (XRF) spectrometer, which excites atoms with a primary X-ray beam and causes secondary (or fluorescent) X-rays to be emitted. Each element produces a diagnostic X-radiation, the intensity of which is measured. This intensity is proportional to the concentration of the element in the rock, and so the bulk composition can be calculated. The crushed powder of the rock is compressed into a disk or fused into a bead and loaded into the spectrometer, which analyzes it automatically under computer control. Analysis of most elements having concentrations of more than five parts per million is possible.

Another important instrument is the induction-coupled plasma (ICP) spectrometer. This instrument can analyze over 40 elements. Here, a solution of a rock is put into a plasma, and the concentration of the elements is determined from the light emitted. This method is rapid, and the ICP spectrometer is particularly suited to analyzing large numbers of soil and stream sediment samples, as well as mineralized rocks in mineral exploration.

THE GEOLOGIC TIME SCALE

The extensive interval of time occupied by the geologic history of Earth is known as geologic time. It extends from about 4.6 billion years ago (corresponding to Earth's initial formation) to the present day. It is, in effect, that segment of Earth history that is represented by and recorded in rock strata.

The geologic time scale is the "calendar" for events in Earth history. It subdivides all time into named units of abstract time called—in descending order of duration—eons, eras, periods, epochs, and ages. The enumeration of those geologic time units is based on stratigraphy, which is the correlation and classification of rock strata. The fossil forms that occur in the rocks provide the chief means of establishing a geologic time scale. Because living things have undergone evolutionary changes over geologic time, particular kinds of organisms are characteristic of particular parts of the geologic record. By correlating the strata in which certain types of fossils are found, the geologic history of various regions—and of Earth as a whole—can be reconstructed. The relative geologic time scale developed from the fossil record has been numerically quantified by means of absolute dates obtained with radiometric dating methods.

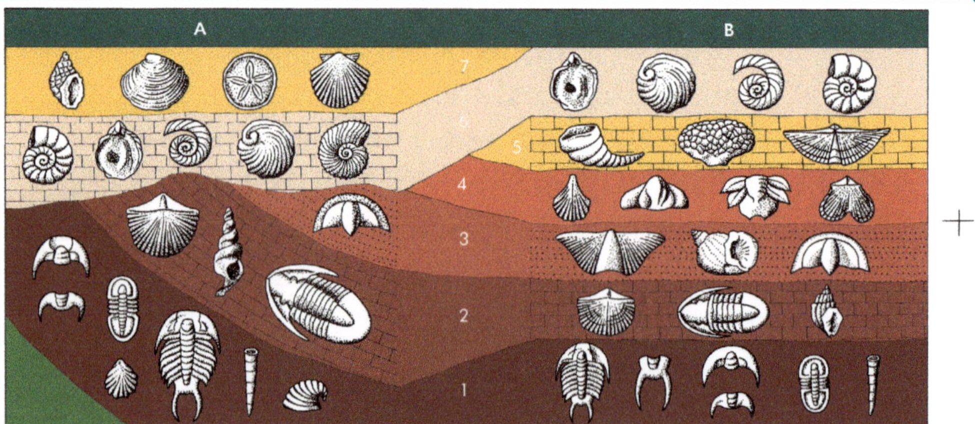

Fossils help geologists establish the ages of layers of rock. In this diagram that illustrates geologic time, sections A and B represent rock layers 200 miles (320 kilometers) apart. Their ages can be established by comparing the fossils in each layer.

ISOTOPIC GEOCHEMISTRY

Isotopic geochemistry has several principal roles in geology. One is concerned with the changes in certain isotopic species that result from the influence of differences in mass of molecules containing different isotopes. Measurements of the proportions of various isotopic species can be used as a form of geologic thermometer. For example, the ratio of the isotopes oxygen-16 to oxygen-18 in the calcium carbonate secreted by various marine organisms from the calcium carbonate in solution in seawater is influenced by the temperature of the seawater. Precise measurement of the proportions of oxygen-16 with respect to oxygen-18 in calcareous shells of some fossil marine organisms provides a means of estimating the temperatures of the seas in which they lived. The varying ocean temperatures during and between the major advances of glaciers during the ice ages have been inferred by analyzing the isotopic composition of the skeletons of floating organisms recovered as fossils in sediment on the seafloor.

Another role of isotopic geochemistry that is of great importance in geology is radiometric age dating. The ability to quantify the geologic time scale—that is, to date the events

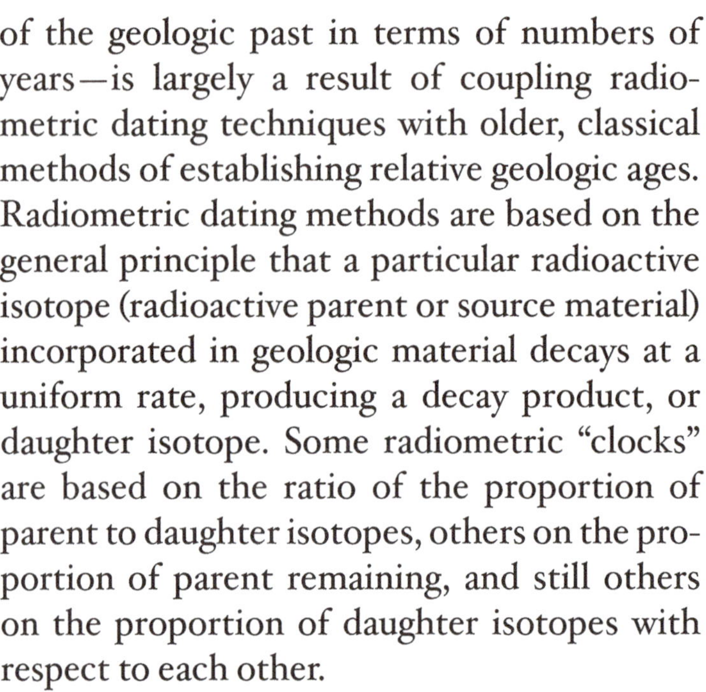

of the geologic past in terms of numbers of years—is largely a result of coupling radiometric dating techniques with older, classical methods of establishing relative geologic ages. Radiometric dating methods are based on the general principle that a particular radioactive isotope (radioactive parent or source material) incorporated in geologic material decays at a uniform rate, producing a decay product, or daughter isotope. Some radiometric "clocks" are based on the ratio of the proportion of parent to daughter isotopes, others on the proportion of parent remaining, and still others on the proportion of daughter isotopes with respect to each other.

For example, uranium-238 decays ultimately to lead-206, which is one of the four naturally occurring isotopic species of lead. Minerals that contain uranium-238 when initially formed may be dated by measuring the proportions of lead-206 and uranium-238; the older the specimen, the greater the proportion of lead-206 with respect to uranium-238. The decay of potassium-40 to argon-40 (calcium-40 is produced in this decay process as well) is also a widely used radiometric dating tool. There are several other parent-daughter pairs that are used in radiometric dating, including another isotope of uranium

(uranium-235), which decays ultimately to form lead-207, and thorium-232, which decays to lead-208.

Uranium-238 and uranium-235 decay very slowly, although uranium-235 decays more rapidly than uranium-238. The rate of decay may be expressed in several ways. One way is by the radioactive isotope's half-life—the interval of time in which half of any given initial amount will have decayed. The half-life of uranium-238 is about 4,510,000,000 years, whereas the half-life of uranium-235 is about 713,000,000 years. Other radioactive isotopes decay at greatly differing rates, with half-lives ranging from a fraction of a second to quadrillions of years.

It is useful to combine a variety of isotopic methods to determine the complete history of a crustal rock. A samarium-147–neodymium-143 date on a sample of granitic gneiss, for example, may be interpreted as the time of mantle–crust differentiation or crustal accretion that produced the original magmatic granite. Also, a lead-207–lead-206 date on a zircon will indicate the crystallization age of the granite.

Since the late 20th century two technological advancements have greatly increased the geologist's ability to compute the isotopic age of rocks and minerals. The SHRIMP

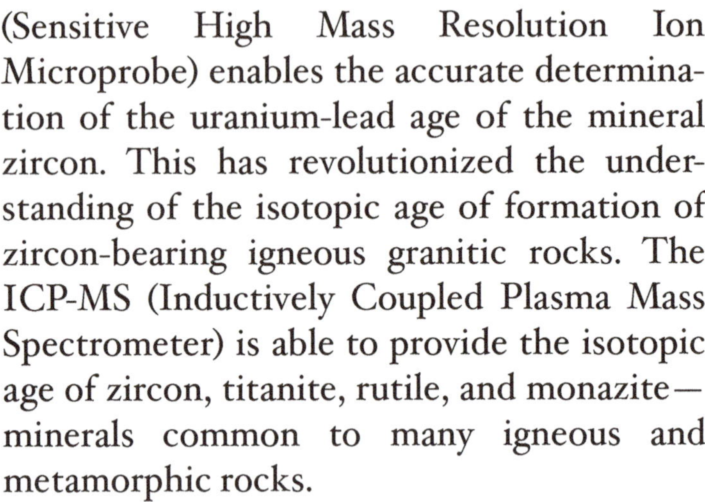

(Sensitive High Mass Resolution Ion Microprobe) enables the accurate determination of the uranium-lead age of the mineral zircon. This has revolutionized the understanding of the isotopic age of formation of zircon-bearing igneous granitic rocks. The ICP-MS (Inductively Coupled Plasma Mass Spectrometer) is able to provide the isotopic age of zircon, titanite, rutile, and monazite—minerals common to many igneous and metamorphic rocks.

An important isotope used to date biological materials is carbon-14, a radioactive isotope of carbon with a half-life of 5,570 years. Carbon-14 is incorporated in all living material, for it is derived either directly or indirectly from its presence in atmospheric carbon dioxide. The moderately short half-life of carbon-14 makes it useful for dating biological materials that are more than a few hundred years old and less than 30,000 years old. It has been used to provide correlation of events within this time span, particularly those of the Pleistocene Epoch involving Earth's most recent ice ages.

CHAPTER 2

THE STUDY OF EARTH'S STRUCTURE

Investigating the structure of Earth encompasses many fields of geology. The subdiscipline of geodesy, for example, focuses on the precise figure of Earth—specifically its size and shape. Until the advent of satellites, all geodesic work was based on land surveys employing a geodesic coordinate system (one used to study the geometry of curved surfaces). It is now possible to use satellites in conjunction with the land-based system to refine knowledge of the Earth's shape and dimensions; this endeavor is sometimes termed satellite geodesy.

The aim of geophysics is to deduce the physical properties of Earth, along with its internal composition, from various physical phenomena. Geophysicists study the Earth's magnetic field, the magnetism remaining in rocks and soils from the time of their formation, the flow of heat within the Earth, the force of gravity, and the movement of seismic waves, which

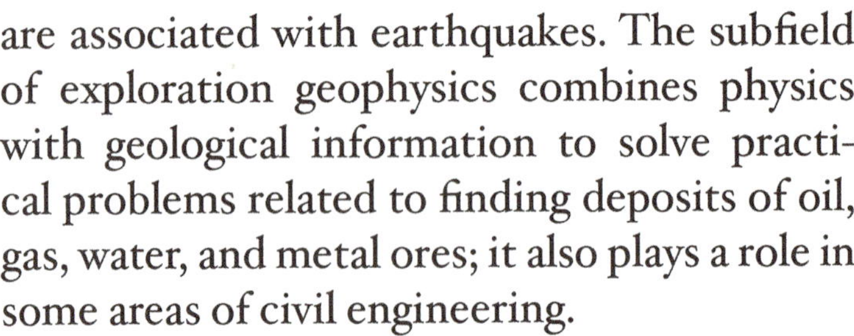

are associated with earthquakes. The subfield of exploration geophysics combines physics with geological information to solve practical problems related to finding deposits of oil, gas, water, and metal ores; it also plays a role in some areas of civil engineering.

Structural geology once was concerned with analyzing the deformation of sedimentary strata, but now structural geologists study the distortions of rocks in general. Commonly investigated structural forms or shapes lead to a comparison of observed features and, eventually, to the classification of related types. Oil and coal geologists employ structural geology in their daily work, especially in petroleum exploration to detect structural traps that can hold petroleum.

In the field of tectonics, geologists study the deformation of the rocks that make up the Earth's crust and the forces that produce such deformation. It deals with the folding and faulting associated with mountain building; the large-scale, gradual upward and downward movements of the crust (epeirogenic movements); and sudden horizontal displacements along faults. Other phenomena studied include igneous processes and metamorphism. Tectonics embraces as its chief working principle the scientific theory of plate tectonics.

Volcanology is the branch of geology that studies volcanoes and volcanic activity. It also deals with the formation, distribution, and classification of volcanoes as well as with their structure and the kinds of materials ejected during an eruption (such as pyroclastic flows, lava, dust, ash, and volcanic gases). A key objective of some areas of volcanology is determining the nature and causes of volcanic eruptions in order to improve forecasting their occurrence.

GEODESY

The scientific objective of geodesy is to determine the size and shape of Earth. The practical role of geodesy is to provide a network of accurately surveyed points on Earth's surface, the vertical elevations and geographic positions of which are precisely known and, in turn, may be incorporated in maps. When two geographic coordinates of a control point on the Earth's surface, its latitude and longitude, are known, as well as its elevation above sea level, the location of that point is known with an accuracy within the limits of error involved in the surveying processes.

In mapping large areas, such as a whole state or country, the irregularities in the curvature

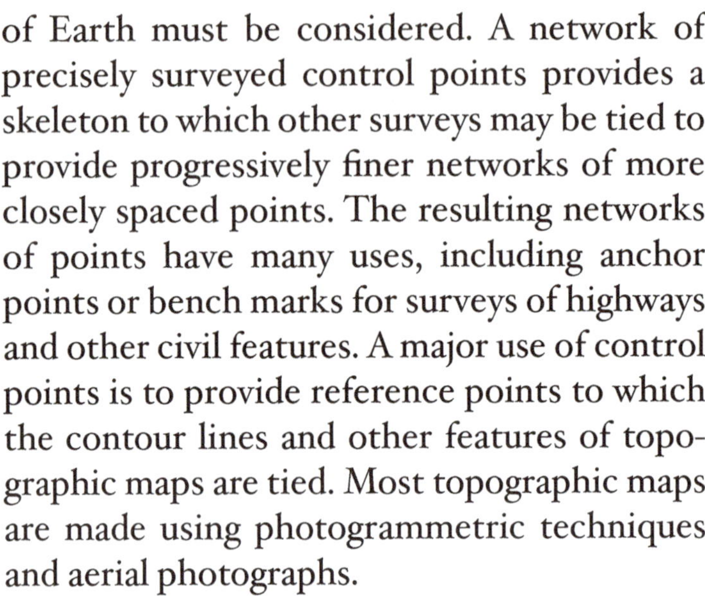

of Earth must be considered. A network of precisely surveyed control points provides a skeleton to which other surveys may be tied to provide progressively finer networks of more closely spaced points. The resulting networks of points have many uses, including anchor points or bench marks for surveys of highways and other civil features. A major use of control points is to provide reference points to which the contour lines and other features of topographic maps are tied. Most topographic maps are made using photogrammetric techniques and aerial photographs.

Earth's figure is that of a surface called the geoid, which over Earth is the average sea level at each location; under the continents the geoid is an imaginary continuation of sea level. The geoid is not a uniform spheroid, however, because of the existence of irregularities in the attraction of gravity from place to place on Earth's surface. These irregularities of the geoid would bring about serious errors in the surveyed location of control points if astronomical methods, which involve use of the local horizon, were used solely in determining locations. Because of these irregularities, the reference surface used in geodesy is that of a regular mathematical surface, an ellipsoid of revolution that fits the geoid as closely as

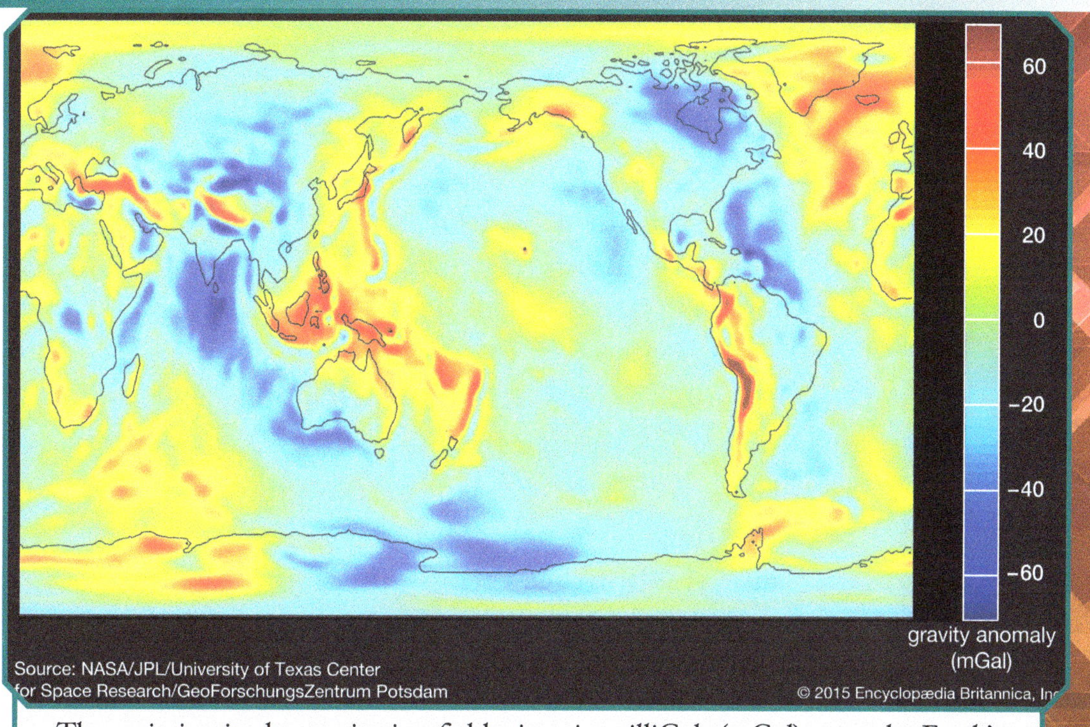

The variation in the gravitation field, given in milliGals (mGal), over the Earth's surface gives rise to an imaginary surface known as the geoid. The geoid expresses the height of an imaginary global ocean not subject to tides, currents, or winds.

possible. This reference ellipsoid is below the geoid in some places and above it in others. Over the oceans, mean sea level defines the geoid surface, but over the land areas the geoid is an imaginary sea-level surface.

Today perturbations in the motions of artificial satellites are used to define the global geoid and gravity pattern with a high degree of accuracy. Geodetic satellites are positioned at a height of 435–497 miles (700–800 kilometers) above Earth. Simultaneous range observations from several laser stations fix the position of a

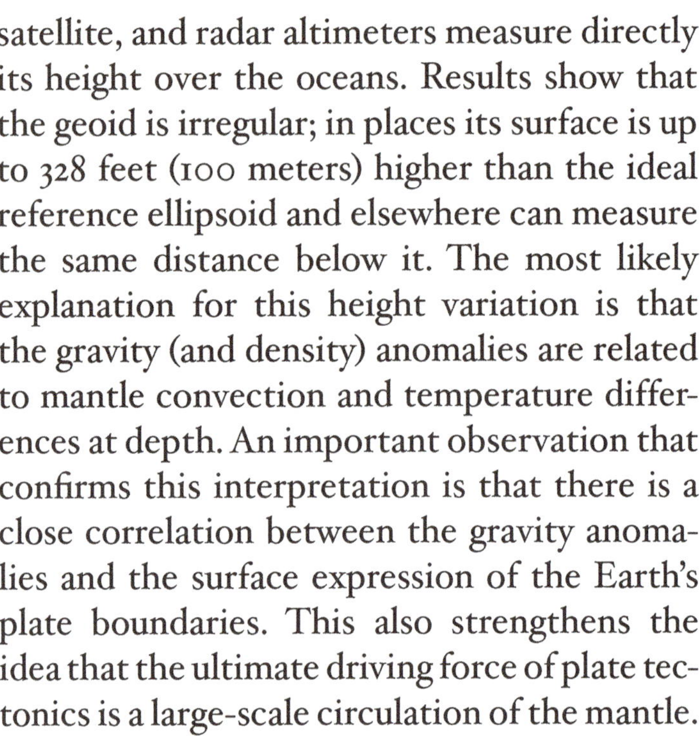

satellite, and radar altimeters measure directly its height over the oceans. Results show that the geoid is irregular; in places its surface is up to 328 feet (100 meters) higher than the ideal reference ellipsoid and elsewhere can measure the same distance below it. The most likely explanation for this height variation is that the gravity (and density) anomalies are related to mantle convection and temperature differences at depth. An important observation that confirms this interpretation is that there is a close correlation between the gravity anomalies and the surface expression of the Earth's plate boundaries. This also strengthens the idea that the ultimate driving force of plate tectonics is a large-scale circulation of the mantle.

A similar satellite ranging technique is also used to determine the drift rates of continents. Repeated measurements of laser light travel times between ground stations and satellites permit the relative movement of different control blocks to be calculated.

GEOPHYSICS

Geophysics pertains to studies of the Earth that involve the methods and principles of physics. The scope of geophysics touches on virtually all aspects of geology, ranging from considerations of the conditions in Earth's deep interior, where temperatures of several thousands of degrees Celsius and pressures of millions of atmospheres prevail, to the Earth's exterior, including its atmosphere and hydrosphere.

The study of the Earth's interior provides a good example of the geophysicist's approach to problems. Direct observation, of course, is impossible. Instead, extensive knowledge of Earth's interior has been derived from a variety of measurements, including seismic waves produced by earthquakes that travel

An officer at the Center for Volcanology and Geological Hazard Mitigation in East Java, Indonesia, measures the maximum amplitude of a seismograph at Bromo Volcano Observation Post in December 2015. Bromo is an active volcano.

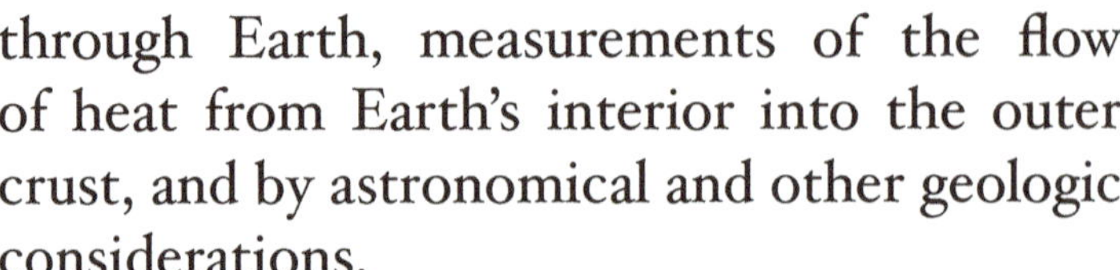

through Earth, measurements of the flow of heat from Earth's interior into the outer crust, and by astronomical and other geologic considerations.

Geophysics may be divided into a number of overlapping branches: (1) study of variations in Earth's gravity field; (2) seismology, the study of Earth's crust and interior by analysis of seismic waves; (3) the physics of the outer atmosphere, with particular attention to the radiation bombardment from the Sun and from outer space, including the influence of Earth's magnetic field on radiation intercepted by the planet; (4) terrestrial electricity, which is the study of the storage and flow of electricity in the atmosphere and the solid Earth; (5) geomagnetism, the study of the source, configuration, and changes in Earth's magnetic field and the study and interpretation of the remanent magnetism in rocks induced by Earth's magnetic field when the rocks were formed (paleomagnetism); (6) the study of Earth's thermal properties, including the temperature distribution of Earth's interior and variations in heat transmission from the interior to the surface; and (7) the convergence of several of these branches for the study of large-scale tectonic structures, such as rifts, continental margins, subduction zones, mid-oceanic ridges, thrusts, and continental sutures.

The techniques of geophysics include measurement of Earth's gravitational field using gravimeters on land and sea and artificial satellites in space; measurement of its magnetic field with hand-held magnetometers or larger units towed behind research ships and aircraft; and seismographic measurement of subsurface structures using reflected and refracted elastic waves generated either by earthquakes or by artificial means (for example, underground nuclear explosions).

Other tools and techniques of geophysics are diverse. Some involve laboratory studies of rocks and other earth materials under high pressures and elevated temperatures. The transmission of elastic waves through the crust and interior of the Earth is strongly influenced by the behavior of materials under the extreme conditions at depth; consequently, there is strong reason to attempt to simulate those conditions of elevated temperatures and pressures in the laboratory. At another extreme, data gathered by rockets and satellites yield much information about radiation flux in space and the magnetic effects of the Earth and other planetary bodies, as well as providing high precision in establishing locations in geodetic surveying, particularly over the oceans.

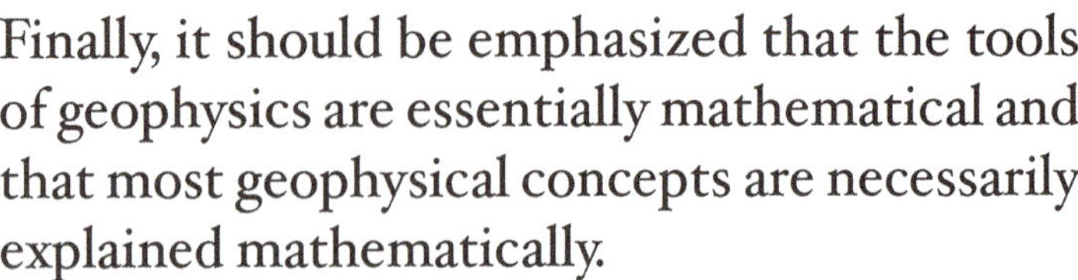

Finally, it should be emphasized that the tools of geophysics are essentially mathematical and that most geophysical concepts are necessarily explained mathematically.

Geophysics has major influence both as a field of pure science (in which the objective is pursuit of knowledge for the sake of knowledge) and as an applied science (in which the objectives involve solving problems of practical or commercial interest). Its principal commercial applications lie in the exploration for oil and natural gas and, to a lesser extent, in the search for metallic ore deposits. Geophysical methods also are used in certain geologic-engineering applications, as in determining the depth of alluvial fill that overlies bedrock, an important factor in the construction of highways and large buildings.

Much of the success of the plate tectonics theory has depended on the corroborative factual evidence provided by geophysical techniques. For example, seismology has demonstrated that the earthquake belts of the world demarcate plate boundaries and that intermediate and deep seismic foci define the dip of subduction zones. The study of rock magnetism has defined the magnetic anomaly patterns of the oceans, and paleomagnetism has charted the drift of continents through geologic time.

STRUCTURAL GEOLOGY

Structural geology deals with the geometric relationships of rocks and geologic features in general. The scope of structural geology is vast, ranging from submicroscopic lattice defects in crystals to mountain belts and plate boundaries.

Structures may be divided into two broad classes: the primary structures that were acquired in the genesis of a rock mass and the secondary structures that result from later deformation of the primary structures. Most layered rocks (sedimentary rocks, some lava flows, and pyroclastic deposits) were deposited initially as nearly horizontal layers. Rocks that were initially horizontal may be deformed later by folding and may be displaced along fractures. If displacement has occurred and the rocks on the two sides of the fracture have moved in opposite directions from each other, the fracture is termed a fault; if displacement has not occurred, the fracture is called a joint.

It is clear that faults and joints are secondary structures; that is to say, their relative age is younger than the rocks that they intersect, but their age may be only slightly younger. Many joints in igneous rocks, for example, were produced by contraction when the rocks

This example of metamorphic slate with folds is located in Nevada. Foliation is the process of dividing rocks, especially metamorphic rocks, into plates or slabs because of the parallel arrangement or cleavage of the minerals.

cooled. On the other hand, some fractures in rocks, including igneous rocks, are related to weathering processes and expansion associated with removal of overlying load. These will have been produced long after the rocks were formed. The faults and joints referred to here are brittle structures that form as discrete fractures within otherwise undeformed rocks in cool upper levels of the crust. In contrast, ductile structures result from permanent changes throughout a wide body of deformed rock at higher temperatures and pressures in deeper crustal levels. Such structures include folds and cleavage in slate belts, foliation in gneisses, and mineral lineation in metamorphic rocks.

The methods of structural geology are diverse. At the smallest scale, lattice defects and dislocations in crystals can be studied in images enlarged several thousand times with transmission electron microscopes. Many structures also can be examined microscopically, using the same general techniques employed in petrology, in which sections of rock mounted on glass slides are ground very thin and are then examined by transmitted light with polarizing microscopes.

On a large scale, the techniques of field geology are employed. These include the preparation of geologic maps that show the areal

FAULTS

In geology, a fault is a planar or gently curved fracture in the rocks of the Earth's crust, where compressional or tensional forces cause relative displacement of the rocks on the opposite sides of the fracture. Faults range in length from a few centimeters to many hundreds of kilometers, and displacement likewise may range from less than a centimeter to several hundred kilometers along the fracture surface (the fault plane). The geographic distribution of faults varies; some large areas have almost none, others are cut by innumerable faults.

Faults may be vertical, horizontal, or inclined at any angle. Although the angle of inclination of a specific fault plane tends to be relatively uniform, it may differ considerably along its length from place to place. When rocks slip past each other in faulting, the upper or overlying block along the fault plane is called the hanging wall, or headwall; the block below is called the footwall. The fault strike is the direction of the line of intersection between the fault plane and the surface of Earth. The dip of a fault plane is its angle of inclination measured from the horizontal.

Faults are classified according to their angle of dip and their relative displacement. Normal dip-slip faults are produced by vertical compression as Earth's crust lengthens. The hanging wall slides down relative to the footwall. Normal faults are common; they bound many of the mountain ranges of the world and many of the rift valleys found along spreading margins of tectonic plates. Rift valleys are formed by the sliding of the hanging walls downward many thousands of meters, where they then become the valley floors.

A block that has dropped relatively downward between two normal faults dipping toward each other is called a graben. A block that has been relatively uplifted between two normal faults that dip away from each other is called a horst. A tilted block that lies between two normal faults dipping in the same direction is a tilted fault block.

Reverse dip-slip faults result from horizontal compressional forces caused by a shortening, or contraction, of the Earth's crust. The hanging wall moves up and over the footwall. Thrust faults are reverse faults that dip less than 45°. Thrust faults with a very low angle of dip and a very large total displacement are called overthrusts or detachments; these are often found in intensely deformed mountain belts.

(continued on the next page)

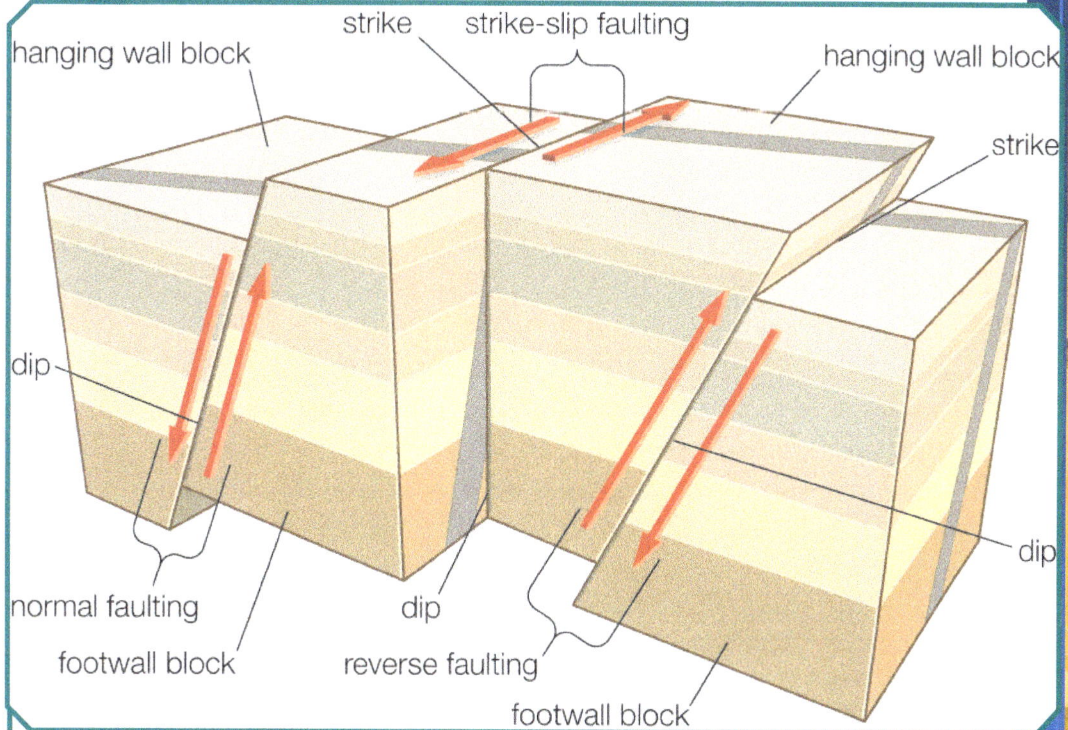

This diagram represents the types of faulting in tectonic earthquakes. In normal and reverse faulting, rock masses slip vertically past each other. In strike-slip faulting, the rocks slip past each other horizontally.

(continued from the previous page)

Large thrust faults are characteristic of compressive tectonic plate boundaries, such as those that have created the Himalayas and the subduction zones along the west coast of South America.

Strike-slip (also called transcurrent, wrench, or lateral) faults are similarly caused by horizontal compression, but they release their energy by rock displacement in a horizontal direction almost parallel to the compressional force. The fault plane is essentially vertical, and the relative slip is lateral along the plane. These faults are widespread. Many are found at the boundary between converging oceanic and continental tectonic plates. A well-known example is the San Andreas Fault in North America; the movement of this fault caused the San Francisco earthquake of 1906.

Oblique-slip faults have simultaneous displacement up or down the dip and along the strike. The displacement of the blocks on the opposite sides of the fault plane usually is measured in relation to sedimentary strata or other stratigraphic markers, such as veins and dikes. The movement along a fault may be rotational, with the offset blocks rotating relative to one another.

Fault slip may polish smooth the walls of the fault plane, marking them with striations called slickensides, or it may crush them to a fine-grained, claylike substance known as fault gouge; when the crushed rock is relatively coarse-grained, it is referred to as fault breccia. Occasionally, the beds adjacent to the fault plane fold or bend as they resist slippage because of friction. Areas of deep sedimentary rock cover often show no surface indications of the faulting below.

Movement of rock along a fault may occur as a continuous creep or as a series of spasmodic jumps of a few meters during a few seconds. Such jumps are separated by intervals during which stress builds up until it overcomes the frictional forces along the fault plane and causes another slip. Most, if not all, earthquakes are caused by rapid slip along faults.

distribution of geologic units selected for representation on the map. They also include the plotting of the orientation of such structural features as faults, joints, cleavage, small folds, and the attitude of beds with respect to three-dimensional space. A common objective is to interpret the structure at some depth below the surface. It is possible to infer with some degree of accuracy the structure beneath the surface by using information available at the surface. If geologic information from drill holes or mine openings is available, the configuration of rocks in the subsurface commonly may be interpreted with much greater assurance as compared with interpretations involving projection to depth based largely on information obtained at the surface.

A combination of structural and geophysical methods are generally used to conduct field studies of large-scale tectonic features. Field

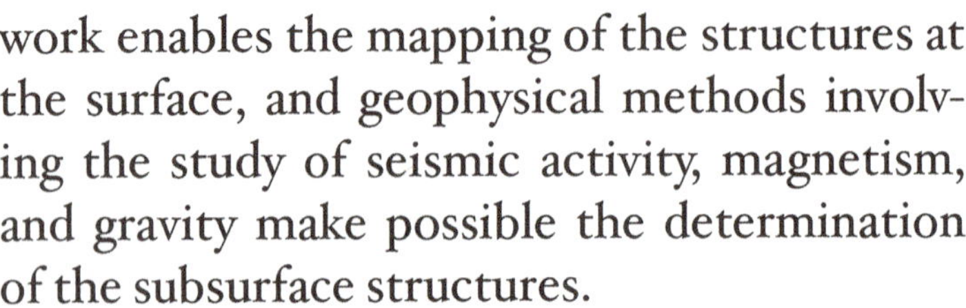

work enables the mapping of the structures at the surface, and geophysical methods involving the study of seismic activity, magnetism, and gravity make possible the determination of the subsurface structures.

The processes that affect geologic structures rarely can be observed directly. The nature of the deforming forces and the manner in which Earth's materials deform under stress can be studied experimentally and theoretically, however, thus providing insight into the forces of nature.

TECTONICS

The subject of tectonics is concerned with Earth's large-scale structural features. It forms a multidisciplinary framework for interrelating many other geologic disciplines, and thus it provides an integrated understanding of large-scale processes that have shaped the development of our planet. These structural features include mid-oceanic rifts; transform faults in the oceans; intracontinental rifts, as in the East African Rift System and on the Tibetan Highlands; faults (for example, the San Andreas Fault in California) that may extend hundreds of kilometers; sedimentary basins; trench systems

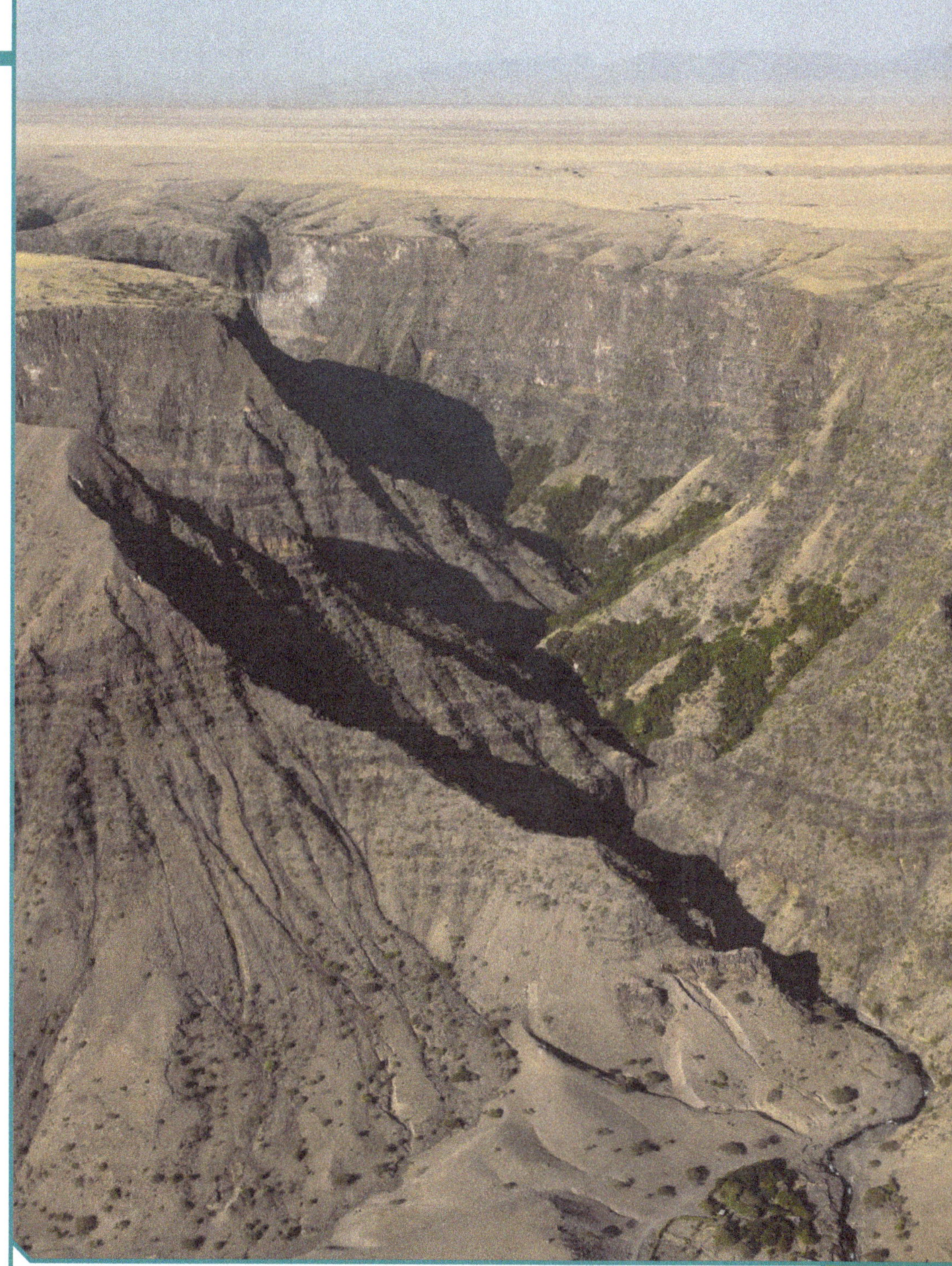

An aerial view depicts a gorge in the East African Rift at Engaruka, Tanzania. This rift system extends from Jordan in southwestern Asia southward through eastern Africa to Mozambique.

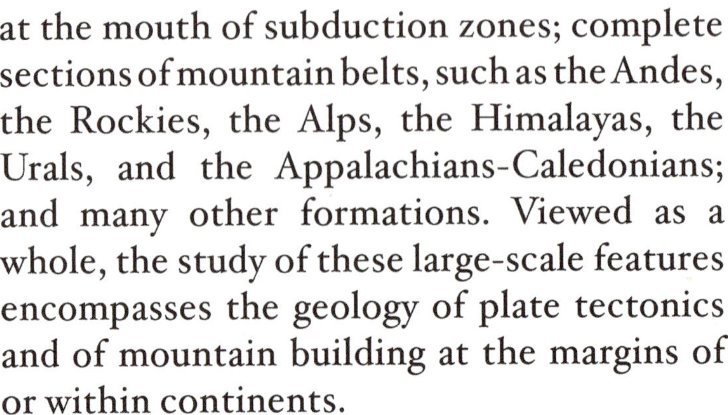

at the mouth of subduction zones; complete sections of mountain belts, such as the Andes, the Rockies, the Alps, the Himalayas, the Urals, and the Appalachians-Caledonians; and many other formations. Viewed as a whole, the study of these large-scale features encompasses the geology of plate tectonics and of mountain building at the margins of or within continents.

VOLCANOLOGY

Volcanology is the science of volcanoes and deals with their structure, petrology, and origin. It is also concerned with the contribution of volcanoes to the development of the Earth's crust, with their role as contributors to the atmosphere and hydrosphere and to the balance of chemical elements in the Earth's crust, and with the relationships of volcanoes to certain forms of metallic ore deposits.

Many of the problems of volcanology are closely related to those of the origin of oceans and continents. Most of the volcanoes of the world are aligned along or close to the major plate boundaries, in particular the mid-oceanic ridges and active continental margins (such as the "Ring of Fire" around the Pacific Ocean). A few volcanoes occur within oceanic plates (for

RING OF FIRE

A seismically active belt of volcanoes and tectonic plate boundaries roughly surrounds the Pacific Ocean. Because the volcanoes frequently erupt in fiery explosions, the belt is known as the Ring of Fire. Many earthquakes occur in the region as well.

For much of its 24,900-mile (40,000-kilometer) length, the Ring of Fire follows chains of islands such as Tonga and Vanuatu, the Indonesian archipelago, the Philippines, Japan, the Kuril Islands, and the Aleutians. The belt also includes the western coast of North America and the Andes Mountains of South America. About three-fourths of the world's volcanoes occur within the Ring of Fire.

The Ring of Fire encapsulates several tectonic plates—these include the vast Pacific Plate and the smaller Philippine, Juan de Fuca, Cocos, and Nazca plates. Earth's plates move at different rates and in different directions. As the Pacific Plate and

(*continued on the next page*)

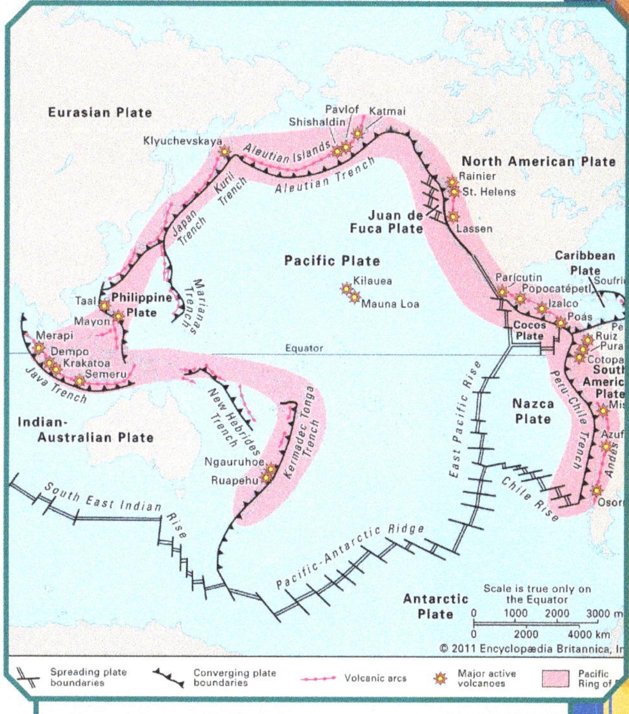

The Ring of Fire is a ring of active volcanoes, volcanic arcs, and tectonic plate boundaries that frame the Pacific Ocean.

(continued from the previous page)

the plates around it grind into each other, they cause earthquakes to occur and volcanoes to erupt.

Major volcanic events that have occurred within the Ring of Fire since 1800 include the eruptions of Mount Tambora (1815), Krakatoa (1883), Novarupta (1912), Mount Saint Helens (1980), Mount Ruiz (1985), and Mount Pinatubo (1991). The Ring of Fire has been the setting for several of the largest earthquakes in recorded history, including the Chile earthquakes of 1960 and 2010, the Alaska earthquake of 1964, and the Japan earthquake of 2011, as well as the earthquake that produced the devastating Indian Ocean tsunami of 2004.

example, along the Hawaiian chain); these are interpreted as the tracks of plumes (ascending jets of partially molten mantle material) that formed when such a plate moved over hot spots fixed in the mantle.

One of the principal reasons for studying volcanoes and volcanic products is that the atmosphere and hydrosphere are believed to be largely derived from volcanic emanations, modified by biological processes. Much of the water present at Earth's surface, which has aggregated mostly in the oceans but to a lesser extent in glaciers, streams, lakes, and groundwater, probably has emerged gradually from Earth's interior by means of volcanoes, beginning very early in Earth's history. The principal components of air—nitrogen and oxygen—probably have been derived through modification of ammonia and carbon dioxide emitted by volcanoes. Emissions of vapors and gases from volcanoes are an aspect of the degassing of Earth's interior. Although the degassing processes that affect Earth were probably much more vigorous when it was newly formed about 4,600,000,000 years ago, it is interesting to consider that the degassing processes are still at work. Their scale, however, is vastly reduced compared with their former intensity.

The study of volcanoes is dependent on a variety of techniques. The petrologic polarizing microscope is used for classifying lava types and for tracing their general mineralogical history. The X-ray fluorescence spectrometer provides a tool for making chemical analyses of rocks that are important for understanding the chemistry of a wide variety of volcanic products (for example, ashes, pumice, scoriae, and bombs) and of the magmas that give rise to them. Some lavas are enriched or depleted in certain isotopic ratios that can be determined with a mass spectrometer. Analyses of gases from volcanoes and of hot springs in volcanic regions provide information about the late stages of volcanic activity. These late stages are characterized by the emission of

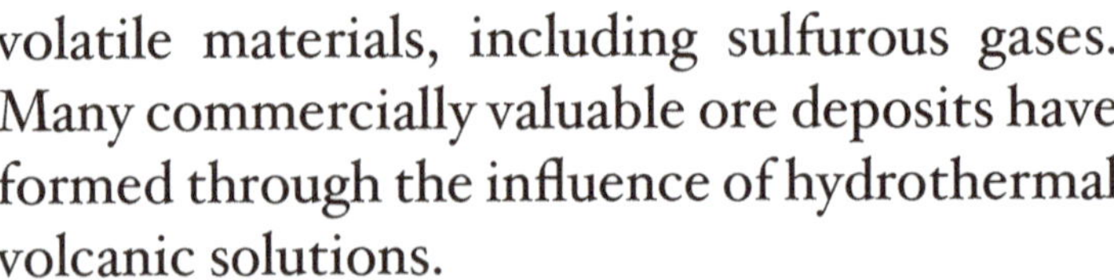

volatile materials, including sulfurous gases. Many commercially valuable ore deposits have formed through the influence of hydrothermal volcanic solutions.

Volcanoes may pose a serious hazard to human life and property, as borne out by the destruction wrought by the eruptions of Mount Vesuvius (79 CE), Krakatoa (1883), Mount Pelée (1902), and Mount Saint Helens (1980), to mention only a few. Because of this, much attention has been devoted to forecasting volcanic outbursts. In 1959 researchers monitored activity leading up to the eruption of Kilauea in Hawaii. Using seismographs, they detected swarms of earthquake tremors for several months prior to the eruption, noting a sharp increase in the number and intensity of small quakes shortly before the outpouring of lava. Tracking such tremors, which are generated by the upward movement of magma from Earth's interior, has proved to be an effective means of determining the onset of eruptions and is now widely used for prediction purposes. Some volcanoes inflate when rising molten rock fills their magma chambers; in such cases tiltmeters can be employed to detect a change in angle of the slope before eruption. Other methods of predicting violent volcanic activity involve the use of laser beams to check for changes in slope, temperature monitors, gas detectors, and instruments sensitive to variations in magnetic and gravity fields. Permanent volcano observatories have been established at some of the world's most active sites such as, Kilauea, Mount Etna, and Mount Saint Helens to ensure early warning.

CHAPTER 3

The Study of Earth's Surface Features and Processes

The study of Earth's features and process allows geologists to develop models that describe the physical features of Earth, and help explain the presence and evolution of these features as a result of the action of glaciers, streams, rivers, windborne dust and sand, and weathering.

Geomorphology

Geomorphology is literally the study of the form or shape of Earth, but it deals principally with the topographical features of Earth's surface. It is concerned with the classification, description, and origin of landforms. The configuration of Earth's surface reflects to some degree virtually all of the processes that take place at or close to the surface as well as those that occur deep in the crust. The intricate details of the shape of a mountain range, for example, result more or less directly from the processes of erosion that progressively remove material from the range. The spectrum of erosive processes includes weathering and soil-forming processes and transportation of materials by running water, wind action, and mass movement.

Glacial processes have been particularly influential in many mountainous regions. These processes are destructional in the sense that they modify and gradually destroy the previous form of the range. Also important in

The Paria River carries sediment from the Grand Canyon downstream and eventually meets the Colorado River in Arizona. Geomorphology deals with the study of erosion, weathering, and the movement of materials by water and wind.

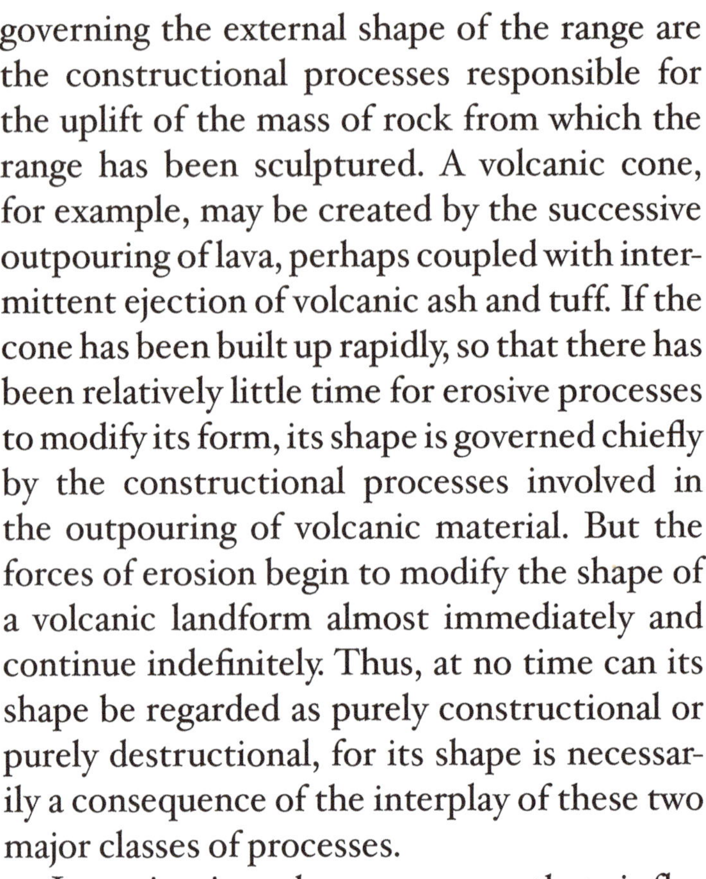

governing the external shape of the range are the constructional processes responsible for the uplift of the mass of rock from which the range has been sculptured. A volcanic cone, for example, may be created by the successive outpouring of lava, perhaps coupled with intermittent ejection of volcanic ash and tuff. If the cone has been built up rapidly, so that there has been relatively little time for erosive processes to modify its form, its shape is governed chiefly by the constructional processes involved in the outpouring of volcanic material. But the forces of erosion begin to modify the shape of a volcanic landform almost immediately and continue indefinitely. Thus, at no time can its shape be regarded as purely constructional or purely destructional, for its shape is necessarily a consequence of the interplay of these two major classes of processes.

Investigating the processes that influence landforms is an important aspect of geomorphology. These processes include the weathering caused by the action of solutions of atmospheric carbon dioxide and oxygen in water on exposed rocks; the activity of streams and lakes; the transport and deposition of dust and sand by wind; the movement of material through downhill creep of soil

Erosion

The process by which soil and rock is removed from one area of the Earth through natural causes such as wind, water, and ice and transported elsewhere is called erosion. In the broadest sense of the word, erosion means the general wearing down and molding of all landforms on Earth's surface.

Moving water is the most important natural agent of erosion. Coastal erosion is mainly brought about by the action of sea waves. Waves drag particles back and forth, abrading the bedrock and each other and gradually wearing pebbles into sand. Wave erosion creates retreating shorelines and etches sea cliffs and arches out of the rock. Sediments are transported by the lateral movement of waves after they wash ashore and lead to advancing shorelines, bars, spits, and barrier beaches. Disintegration or degradation of sea cliffs by natural occurrences such as rain, frost, and tidal scour also partly contributes to erosion.

In rivers the erosion of banks is caused by the scouring action of the moving water, particularly in times of flood. This scouring action draws in and transports sediments within the river or stream. The sediments cause erosion as they abrade one another as they move through the water or as they abrade other rock and soil as they are dragged along the river bottom. As long as the river's volume and velocity increases, more sediment is picked up and moved. As the velocity of the river decreases, the suspended sediments are deposited, creating landforms such as floodplains, sandbars, and river deltas. Land away from rivers and streams is also subjected to a continuous process of erosion through the action of rain, snowmelt, and frost.

Glacial erosion occurs in two principal ways: through the abrasion of surface materials as the ice grinds over the

(continued on the next page)

Margerie Glacier in Glacier Bay National Park in Alaska displays layers and folds that contain rocks and other debris in ice. The layers of rock were buried by snow and then folded as they moved down slopes.

(*continued from the previous page*)

ground (much of the abrasive action is caused by the debris embedded in the ice along its base); and by the quarrying or plucking of rock from the glacier bed. The eroded material is transported until it is deposited or until the glacier melts.

In some desert areas, wind brings about the erosion of rocks by driving sand. In addition, the surface of sand dunes not held together and protected by vegetation is subject to erosion and change by the drifting of blown sand. The wind not only removes small loose particles, leaving larger particles behind, but also sandblasts the landforms by wind-transported material. The material continues to blow around until the wind lessens or until the wind-blown particles collide with or cling to a surface feature.

and rock and by landslides and mudflows; and shoreline processes that involve the mechanics and effects of waves and currents. Study of these different types of processes forms subdisciplines that exist more or less in their own right.

Glacial Geology

Glacial geology can be regarded as a branch of geomorphology, though it is such a large area of research that it stands as a distinct subdiscipline within the geologic sciences. Glacial geology is concerned with the properties of glaciers themselves as well as with the effects of glaciers as agents of both erosion and deposition.

Glaciers are accumulations of snow transformed into solid ice. Important questions of glacial geology concern the climatic controls that influence the occurrence of glaciers, the processes by which snow is transformed into ice, and the mechanism of the flow of ice within glaciers. Other important questions involve the manner in which glaciers serve as erosive agents, not only in mountainous regions but also over large regions where great continental glaciers now extend or once existed. Much of

A glacier is sandwiched between Bettelmatthorn and Rothorn mountains near Nufenen Pass in Ulrichen, Switzerland. The Alpine peaks were made of large complexes of massed overthrusts of extremely varied rocks that were shaped by glaciation.

the topography of the northern part of North America and Eurasia, for example, has been strongly influenced by glaciers. In places, bedrock has been scoured of most surficial debris. Elsewhere, deposits of glacial till mantle much of the area. Other extensive deposits include unconsolidated sediments deposited in former lakes that existed temporarily as a result of dams created by glacial ice or by glacial deposits. Many presently existing lakes are of glacial origin as, for example, the Great Lakes.

The Geology of the Great Lakes

The Great Lakes constitute a chain of deep freshwater lakes in east-central North America comprising Lakes Superior, Michigan, Huron, Erie, and Ontario. They are one of the great natural features of the continent and of Earth. Although Lake Baikal in Russia has a larger volume of water, the combined area of the Great Lakes—some 94,250 square miles (244,106 square kilometers)—represents the largest surface of fresh water in the world, covering an area exceeding that of the United Kingdom.

The age of the Great Lakes is not definitely determined. Estimates range from 7,000 to 32,000 years of age. Water began filling the glacially scoured basins as soon as the ice receded, some 14,000 years ago. It is generally accepted that Lake Erie reached its present level about 10,000 years ago, Lake Ontario about 7,000 years ago, and Lakes Huron, Michigan, and Superior some 3,000 years ago.

The present configuration of the Great Lakes basin is the result of the movement of massive glaciers through the mid-continent, a process that began about one million years ago during the Pleistocene Epoch. Studies in the Lake Superior region indicate that a river system and valleys formed by water erosion existed before the Ice Age. The glaciers undoubtedly scoured these valleys, widening and deepening them and radically changing the drainage of the area.

The last glaciation in North America is called the Wisconsin Glacial Stage because it left many fresh landforms and sediments in that state. As the ice sheet melted and receded about 14,000 years ago, the first segments of

(continued on the next page)

Landsat satellites, which were designed to collect information on natural resources and other Earth features, compiled data to make this image of the Great Lakes. The basins of the five lakes were probably scooped out by the Ice Age glaciers.

(continued from the previous page)

the Great Lakes were created. Lake Chicago, in what is now the southern Lake Michigan basin, and Lake Maumee, in present-day western Lake Erie and its adjacent lowlands, originally drained southward into the Mississippi River through the Illinois and Wabash drainages, respectively. As the ice retreat continued, Lake Maumee was drained into Lake Chicago through a valley that now contains the Grand River in Michigan. Eventually, drainage to the east and into the Atlantic Ocean was established, at one time

down the valleys of the Mohawk and Hudson rivers and then along the course of the upper St. Lawrence River. At one high-water stage, the waters of the Huron and Michigan basin formed one large lake—Lake Algonquin. At the same time, Lake Duluth, in the western Lake Superior basin, also drained to the Mississippi.

The weight of the ice sheet exerted enormous pressures on Earth's crust. As the ice sheet retreated, low-lying, glacially depressed areas, such as the region to the east of Georgian Bay, were exposed. About 10,000 years ago, the upper lakes discharged through this area via the Ottawa River valley, and their levels were substantially reduced. After the weight of the ice was removed, the land (namely, the outlet to the lakes) began to rise, closing off some outlets and allowing the water levels of the lakes to slowly rise. The largest postglacial lake, Nipissing, occupied the basins of Huron, Michigan, and Superior. Drainage through the Ottawa River valley ceased, and outflow from the upper lakes was established by way of the St. Clair and Detroit rivers into Lake Erie. Uplift has continued at a rate of about 1 foot (30 centimeters) every 100 years; this is evidenced by the drowned river mouths of western Lakes Erie and Superior.

A wide range of rock types and deposits are found in the Great Lakes because of their broad area and glacial origin. The ancient rocks of the Canadian Shield cover part of the Superior and Huron basins, while Paleozoic sedimentary rocks make up the remainder of the basins. There are limestone outcrops and large deposits of sand and gravel, usually near shore. Glacial clays and organic sediments occur in the deep areas.

Richardson Highway runs along Summit Lake and the Gulkana Glacier in Alaska. Geologists with the US Geological Survey have been studying climate and glacier-related hydrology around Gulkana Glacier since the late 1950s.

Research in glacial geology is conducted with a variety of tools. Investigators use, for example, radar techniques to determine the thickness of glaciers. In order to calculate the progressive advance or retreat of glacial masses, scientists use isotopic analyses to ascertain the age of organic materials associated with glacial moraines.

Other branches of the geologic sciences are closely linked with glacial geology. In glaciated regions the problems of hydrology and hydrogeology are strongly influenced by the presence of glacial deposits. Furthermore, the suitability of glacial deposits as sites for buildings, roads, and other man-made features is influenced by the mechanical properties of the deposits and by soils formed on them.

Chapter 4

Earth's History

By the late 19th century, geologists and biologists had collected evidence suggesting that Earth is at least hundreds of millions of years old, much older than had earlier been thought. Geologists reasoned that vast stretches of time were needed for the slow work of erosion and sedimentation to have had the effects they apparently had. Biologists felt that a similarly long time was needed for evolution to have resulted in the great diversity of life seen today.

The fields of geology that study Earth's history and processes include historical geology, stratigraphy, paleontology and its subfields, and astrogeology. The latter field deals with the composition and structure of planets, asteroids, and other solid bodies in the solar system, and helps scientists to learn about Earth's development.

HISTORICAL GEOLOGY AND STRATIGRAPHY

One of the major objectives of geology is to establish the history of Earth from its inception to the present. The most important evidence from which geologic history can be inferred is provided by the geometric relationships of rocks with respect to each other, particularly layered rocks, or strata, the relative ages of which may be determined by applying simple principles. A major principle of stratigraphy is that within a sequence of layers of sedimentary

Steno's laws of stratigraphy

1.

Law of superposition
Younger layers of rock sit atop older layers.

2.

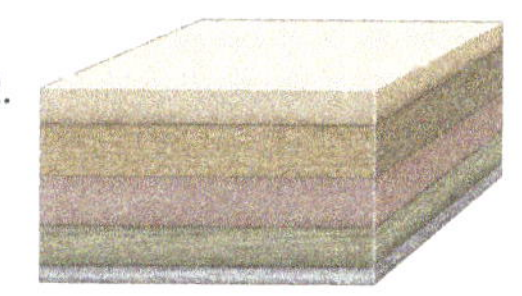

A. Original orientation

B. Orientation after tilting (folding)

Law of original horizontality
Layers of sedimentary rock are originally deposited flat.

3.

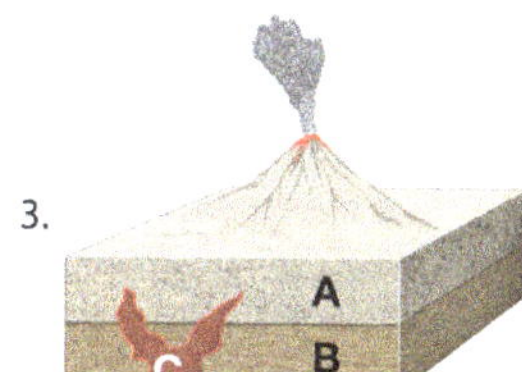

Law of cross-cutting relationships
Rock layers A and B must be older than the intrusion (C) that disturbs them.

4.

Law of lateral continuity
Layers of rock are continuous until they encounter other solid bodies that block their deposition or until they are acted upon by agents that appeared after deposition took place.

Nicolaus Steno, a 17th-century Danish geologist, laid out several propositions for the superposition of rock strata. Steno's laws of stratigraphy describe the patterns in which rock layers are deposited.

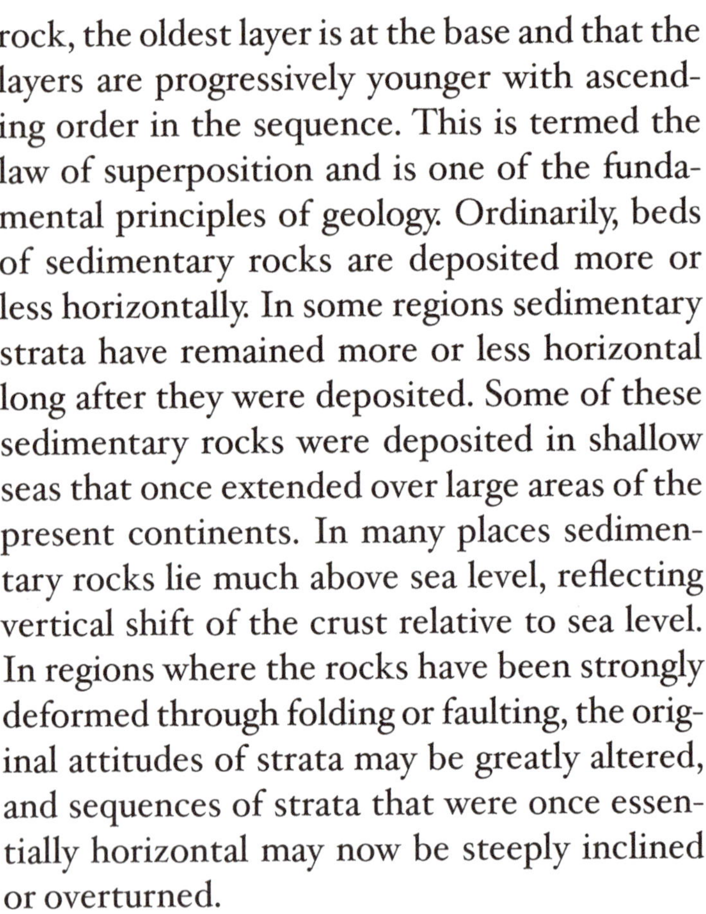

rock, the oldest layer is at the base and that the layers are progressively younger with ascending order in the sequence. This is termed the law of superposition and is one of the fundamental principles of geology. Ordinarily, beds of sedimentary rocks are deposited more or less horizontally. In some regions sedimentary strata have remained more or less horizontal long after they were deposited. Some of these sedimentary rocks were deposited in shallow seas that once extended over large areas of the present continents. In many places sedimentary rocks lie much above sea level, reflecting vertical shift of the crust relative to sea level. In regions where the rocks have been strongly deformed through folding or faulting, the original attitudes of strata may be greatly altered, and sequences of strata that were once essentially horizontal may now be steeply inclined or overturned.

Prior to the development of radiometric methods of dating rocks, the ages of rocks and other geologic features could not be expressed quantitatively, or as numbers of years. Instead, they were expressed solely in terms of relative ages, in which the age of a particular geologic feature could be expressed as relatively younger or older than other geologic features. The ages of different sequences of strata, for example, can be compared with each other in this manner, and their relative ages with respect to faults, igneous intrusions, and other features that exhibit crosscutting relationships can be established. Given such a network of relative ages, a chronology of events has been gradually established in which the relative time of origin of various geologic features is known.

This is the main thread of historical geology—an ordered sequence of geologic events whose occurrence and relative ages have been inferred from evidence preserved in the rocks. In turn, the development of radiometric dating methods has permitted numerical estimates of age to be incorporated in the scale of geologic time.

The development of the mass spectrometer has provided researchers with a means of calculating quantitative ages for rocks throughout the whole of the geologic record. With the aid of various radiometric methods involving mass spectrometric analysis, researchers have found it possible to determine how long ago a particular sediment was deposited, when an igneous rock crystallized or when a metamorphic rock recrystallized, and even the time at which rocks in a mountain belt cooled or underwent uplift.

Radiometric dating also helped geochronologists discover the vast span of geologic time.

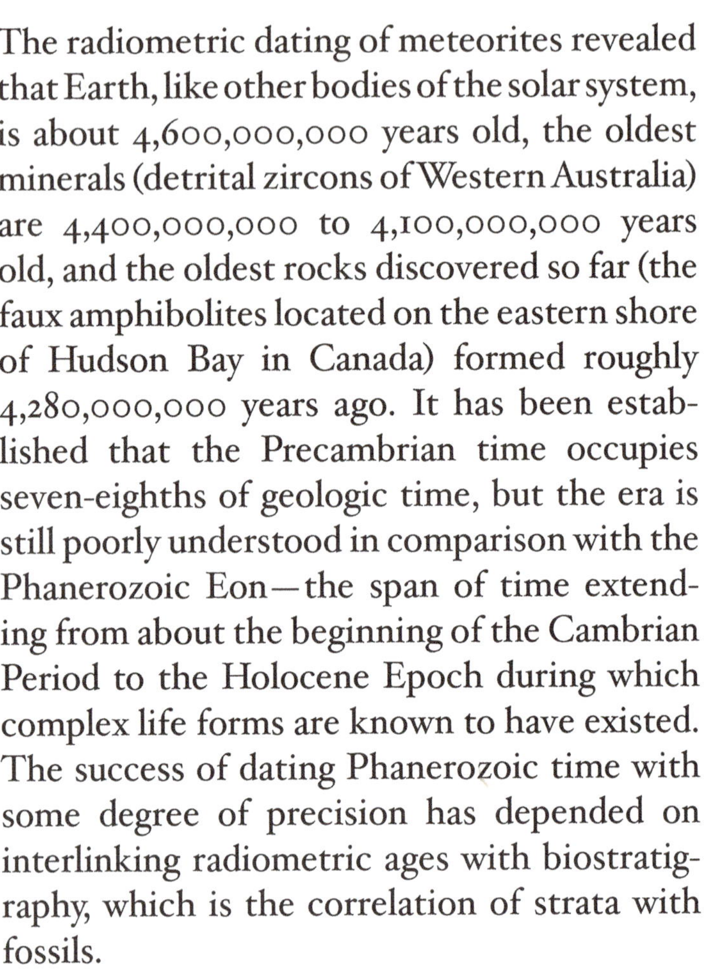

The radiometric dating of meteorites revealed that Earth, like other bodies of the solar system, is about 4,600,000,000 years old, the oldest minerals (detrital zircons of Western Australia) are 4,400,000,000 to 4,100,000,000 years old, and the oldest rocks discovered so far (the faux amphibolites located on the eastern shore of Hudson Bay in Canada) formed roughly 4,280,000,000 years ago. It has been established that the Precambrian time occupies seven-eighths of geologic time, but the era is still poorly understood in comparison with the Phanerozoic Eon—the span of time extending from about the beginning of the Cambrian Period to the Holocene Epoch during which complex life forms are known to have existed. The success of dating Phanerozoic time with some degree of precision has depended on interlinking radiometric ages with biostratigraphy, which is the correlation of strata with fossils.

PALEONTOLOGY

The geologic time scale is based principally on the relative ages of sequences of sedimentary strata. Establishing the ages of strata within a region, as well as the ages of strata in other regions and on different continents, involves stratigraphic correlation from place to place. Although correlation of strata over modest distances often can be accomplished by tracing particular beds from place to place, correlation over long distances and over the oceans almost invariably involves comparison of fossils. With rare exceptions, fossils occur only in sedimentary strata. Paleontology, which is the science of ancient life and deals with fossils, is mutually interdependent with stratigraphy and with historical geology. Paleontology also may be considered to be a branch of biology.

A paleontologist at the Denver Museum of Nature and Science holds a tree leaf fossil from a 64-million-year-old rainforest tree found in rocks near Castle Rock, Colorado. Paleontology is the study of prehistoric life and plant and animal fossils.

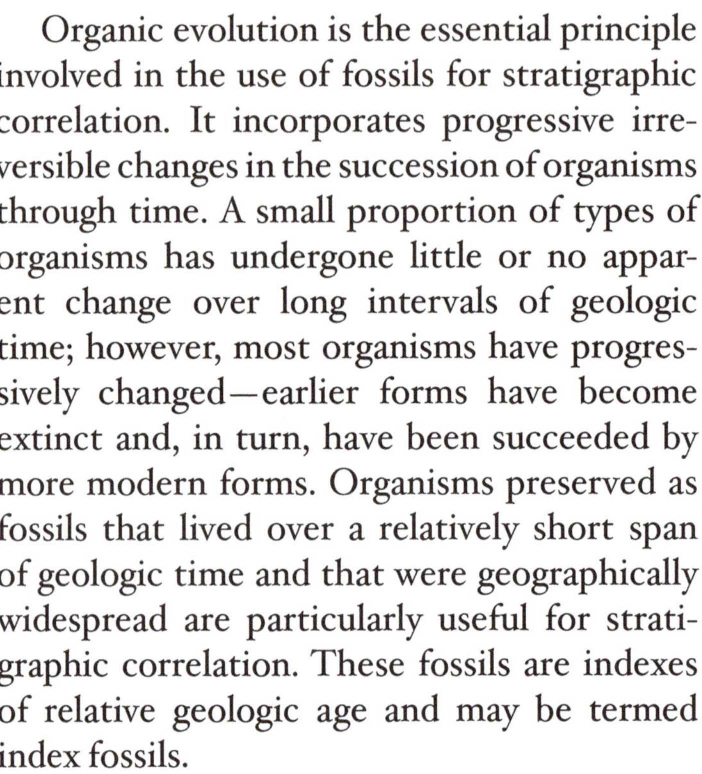

Organic evolution is the essential principle involved in the use of fossils for stratigraphic correlation. It incorporates progressive irreversible changes in the succession of organisms through time. A small proportion of types of organisms has undergone little or no apparent change over long intervals of geologic time; however, most organisms have progressively changed—earlier forms have become extinct and, in turn, have been succeeded by more modern forms. Organisms preserved as fossils that lived over a relatively short span of geologic time and that were geographically widespread are particularly useful for stratigraphic correlation. These fossils are indexes of relative geologic age and may be termed index fossils.

Fossils play another major role in geology because they serve as indicators of ancient environments. Specialists called paleoecologists seek to determine the environmental conditions under which a fossil organism lived and the physical and biological constraints on those conditions. Did the organism live in the seas, lakes, or bogs? In what type of biological community did it live? What was its food chain? In short, what ecological niche did the organism occupy? Because oil and natural gas only accumulate in certain environments,

THE FOSSIL RECORD

The fossil record is the history of life as documented by fossils, the remains or imprints of the organisms from earlier geological periods preserved in sedimentary rock. In a few cases the original substance of the hard parts of the organism is preserved, but more often the original components have been replaced by minerals deposited from water seeping through the rock. Occasionally the original material is simply removed, while nothing is deposited in its place; in this case, all that remains is a mold of the shape of the plant or animal.

In some places, such as the Grand Canyon in Arizona, it is possible to recognize a great thickness of nearly horizontal strata representing the deposition of sediment on the seafloor over many hundreds of millions of years. It is often observed that each layer in such a sequence contains fossils that are distinct from those of the layers that are above and below it. In such sequences of layers in different places, the same, or similar, fossil floras or faunas occur in the same order. By comparing overlapping sequences it is possible to build up a continuous record of faunas or floras that have progressively more in common with present-day life forms as the top of the sequence is approached.

Study of the fossil record has provided important information for at least three different purposes. The progressive changes observed within an animal group are used to describe the evolution of that group. In general, but not always, successive generations tend to change morphologically in a particular direction (for example, the progressive acquisition or loss of specific features), and these changes are often interpreted as better adaptation (through natural

(*continued on the next page*)

(*continued from the previous page*)

selection of beneficial variations in a trait) to a particular environment.

Fossils also provide the geologist a quick and easy way of assigning an age to the strata in which they occur. The precision with which this may be done in any particular case depends on the nature and abundance of the fauna: some fossil groups were deposited during much longer time intervals than others.

Fossil organisms, furthermore, may provide useful information about the climate and environment of the site where they were deposited and preserved. Certain species of coral, for example, require warm, shallow water; certain plants require warm, swampy conditions such as are found today in the Florida Everglades. Thus, when rocks containing fossils of this kind are found in rocks of the present-day polar regions, there is a strong presumption that the crust on which they were deposited has shifted its position on the surface of Earth since that time.

paleoecology can offer useful information for fossil fuel exploration.

INVERTEBRATE PALEONTOLOGY

One of the major branches of paleontology is invertebrate paleontology, which is principally concerned with fossil marine invertebrate animals large enough to be seen with little or no magnification. The number of invertebrate fossil forms is large and includes brachiopods, pelecypods, cephalopods, gastropods, corals and other coelenterates (for example, jellyfish), bryozoans, sponges, and various arthropods (invertebrates with limbs, such as insects), including trilobites, echinoderms, and many other forms, some of which have no living counterparts. The invertebrates that are used as index fossils generally possess hard parts, a characteristic that has fostered their preservation as fossils. The hard parts preserved include the calcareous or chitinous shells of the brachiopods, cephalopods, pelecypods, and gastropods, the jointed exoskeletons of such arthropods as trilobites, and the calcareous skeletons of frame-building corals and bryozoans. The vast variety of organisms lacking hard parts are poorly represented in the geologic record; however, they sometimes occur as impressions or carbonized films in finely laminated sediments.

VERTEBRATE PALEONTOLOGY

Vertebrate paleontology is concerned with fossils of the vertebrates: fish, amphibians, reptiles, birds, and mammals. Although vertebrate paleontology has close ties with stratigraphy, vertebrate fossils usually have not been extensively used as index fossils for stratigraphic correlation mainly because vertebrates generally are much larger than invertebrate fossils and consequently rarer. Fossil mammals, however, have been widely used as index fossils for correlating certain nonmarine strata deposited during the Paleogene Period (about 65.5 to 23 million years ago). Interest in dinosaurs has arisen because of the evidence that they became extinct roughly 65.5 million years ago (at the Cretaceous-Tertiary boundary) during the aftermath of a large meteorite or comet impact.

Paleontologists in 2014 examine the remains of a 12,000-year-old glyptodont, an extinct giant mammal related to modern armadillos, near Padilla, Boliva. Glyptodont fossils have been uncovered there because of wind erosion.

MICROPALEONTOLOGY

Micropaleontology involves the study of organisms so small that they can be observed only with the aid of a microscope. The size range of microscopic fossils, however, is immense. In most cases, the term micropaleontology connotes that aspect of paleontology devoted to the three groups: Ostracoda, a subclass of crustaceans that are generally less than one millimeter in length; Radiolaria, marine protozoans whose remains are common in deep ocean-floor sediments; and Foraminifera, marine protozoans that range in size from about 10 centimeters to a fraction of a millimeter.

Generally speaking, micropaleontology involves successive ranges of sizes of microscopic fossils down to organisms that must be magnified hundreds of times or more for viewing. The study of ultrasmall fossils is perhaps the fastest growing segment of contemporary paleontology and is dependent on modern laboratory instruments, including electron microscopes. It is an important aspect of oil and natural gas exploration. Microfossils, which are flushed up in boreholes in the drilling mud, can be analyzed to determine the depositional environment of the underlying sedimentary

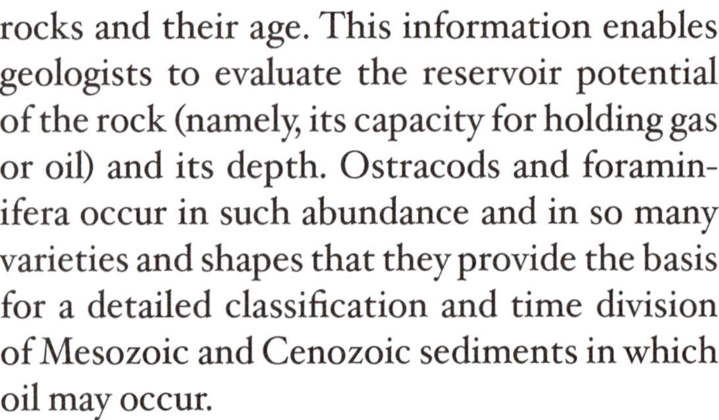

rocks and their age. This information enables geologists to evaluate the reservoir potential of the rock (namely, its capacity for holding gas or oil) and its depth. Ostracods and foraminifera occur in such abundance and in so many varieties and shapes that they provide the basis for a detailed classification and time division of Mesozoic and Cenozoic sediments in which oil may occur.

Filamentous and spheroidal microfossils are important in many Precambrian sediments. They occur in rocks as old as 3,500,000,000 years and are thus an important testimony of early life on Earth.

PALEOBOTANY

Paleobotany is the study of fossil plants. The oldest widely occurring fossils are various forms of calcareous algae that apparently lived in shallow seas, although some may have lived in freshwater. Their variety is so profuse that their study forms an important branch of paleobotany. Other forms of fossil plants consist of land plants or of plants that lived in swamp forests, standing in water that was fresh or may have been brackish, such as the coal-forming swamps of the Late Carboniferous Period (from about 323,000,000 to 298,000,000 years ago).

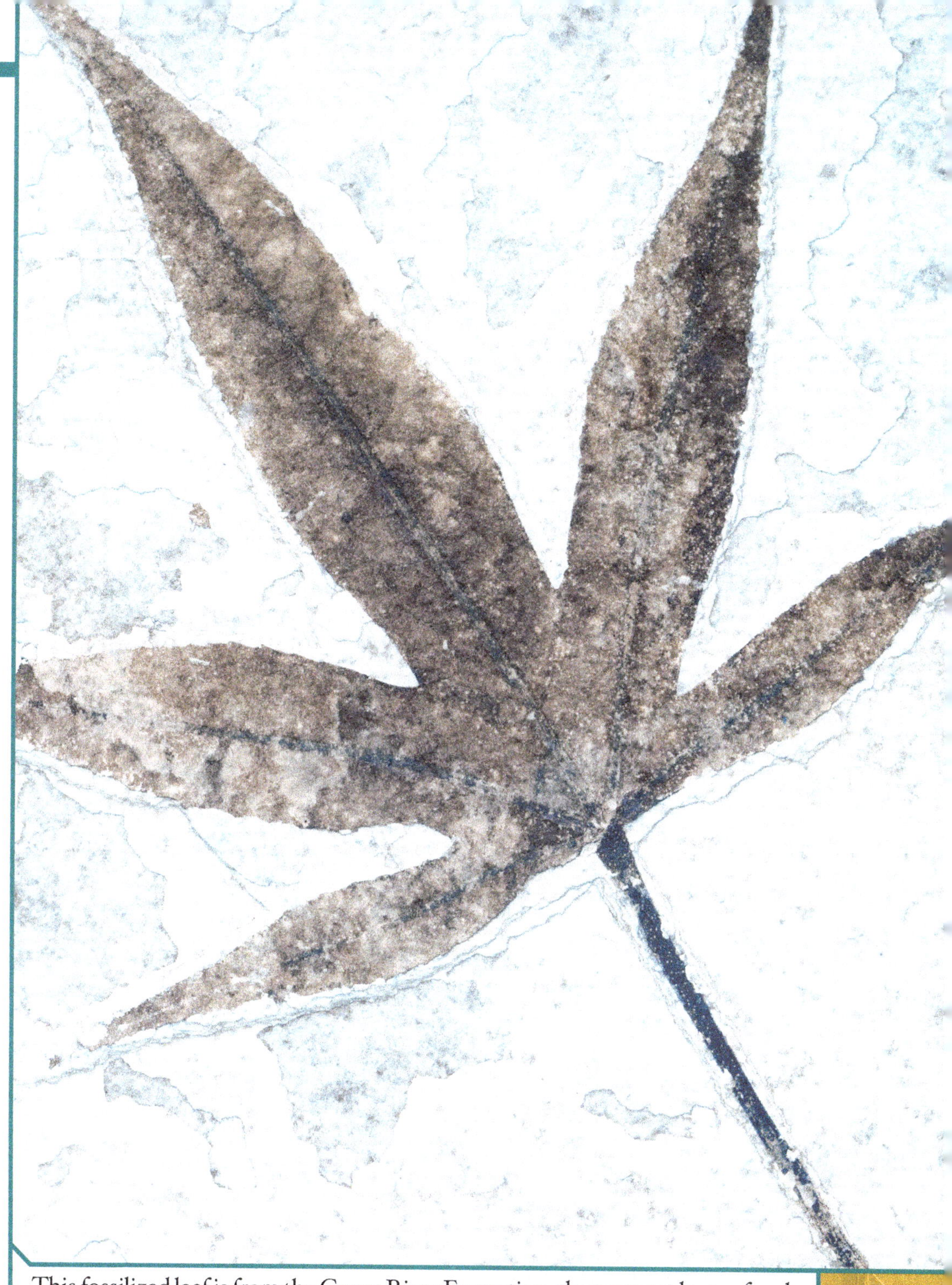

This fossilized leaf is from the Green River Formation, the topmost layer of rock on Fossil Butte in Wyoming. Paleobotanists study changes recorded in plant fossils and have been able to trace much of the evolutionary development of plants.

Palynology

Palynology deals with plant spores and pollen that are both ancient and modern and is a branch of paleobotany. It plays an important role in the investigation of ancient climates, particularly through studies of deposits formed during glacial and interglacial stages. Study of a sequence of spore- or pollen-bearing beds may reveal successive climatic changes, as indicated by changes in types of spores and pollen derived from different vegetative complexes. Spores and pollen are borne by the wind and spread over large areas. Furthermore, they tend to be resistant to decay and thus may be preserved in sediments under adverse conditions.

Astrogeology

Astrogeology is concerned with the geology of the solid bodies in the solar system, such as the asteroids and the planets and their moons. Research in this field helps scientists to better understand the evolution of the Earth in comparison with that of its neighbors in the solar system. This subject was once the domain of astronomers, but the advent of spacecraft has made it accessible to geologists, geophysicists, and geochemists. The success of this field of study has depended largely on the development of advanced instrumentation.

The US Apollo program enabled humans to land on the Moon several times since 1969. Rocks were collected, geophysical experiments were set up on the lunar surface, and geophysical measurements were made from spacecraft. The Soyuz program of the Soviet Union also collected much geophysical data from orbiting spacecraft. The mineralogy, petrology, geochemistry, and geochronology of lunar rocks were studied in detail, and this research made it possible to work out the geochemical evolution of the Moon. The various manned and unmanned missions to the Moon resulted in many other accomplishments: for example, a lunar stratigraphy was constructed, geologic maps at a scale of 1:1,000,000 were prepared, and the structure of various features, such as maria, rilles, and craters, was studied. Gravity profiles across the dense, lava-filled maria were produced. The distribution of heat-producing radioactive elements, such as uranium and thorium, was mapped with gamma-ray spectrometers. The Moon's internal structure was determined on the basis of seismographic

The Pathfinder spacecraft was launched by NASA in 1996 to explore the surface of Mars. Its robot rover, named Sojourner, is pictured here exploring Martian rocks. Astrogeology deals with the geologic study of planets and other celestial bodies.

records of moonquakes; the heat flow from the interior was measured, and the day and night temperatures at the surface were recorded.

Since the late 1960s, unmanned spacecraft have been sent to the neighboring planets. Several of these probes were soft-landed on Mars and Venus. Soil scoops from the Martian surface have been chemically analyzed by an on-board X-ray fluorescence spectrometer. The radioactivity of the surface materials of both Mars and Venus have been studied with a gamma-ray detector, the isotopic composition of their atmospheres analyzed with a mass spectrometer, and their magnetic fields measured. Relief and geologic maps of Mars have been made from high-resolution photographs and topographical maps of Venus compiled from radar data transmitted by orbiting spacecraft. Photographs of Mars and Mercury show that their surfaces are studded with many meteorite craters similar to those on the Moon. Detailed studies have been made of the craters, volcanic landforms, lava flows, and rift valleys on Mars, and a simplified geologic-thermal history has been constructed for the planet.

By the late 20th century the United States had sent interplanetary probes past Jupiter, Saturn, and Uranus. The craft transmitted data and high-resolution photographs of these outer planetary systems, including their rings and satellites.

This research has given increased impetus to the study of tektites, meteorites, and meteorite craters on Earth. The mineralogy, geochemistry, and isotopic age of meteorites and tektites have been studied in detail. Meteorites are very old and probably originated in the asteroid belt between Mars and

Jupiter, whereas tektites are very young and most likely formed from material ejected from terrestrial meteorite craters. Many comparative studies have been made of the development and shapes of meteorite craters on Earth, the Moon, Mars, and Mercury. Space exploration has given birth to a new science—the geology of the solar system. Earth can now be understood within the framework of planetary evolution.

Chapter 5

Practical Applications

Geology has numerous practical applications today that are beneficial to society. Discoveries in geological research over the past several decades have resulted in greater scientific understanding of Earth's history and the forces and processes that have shaped Earth's surface and interior. Industries use the results of geological research to mine mineral resources and extract energy sources to their advantage. Civil engineers who grapple with infrastructure projects such as bridges, roads, and buildings benefit from geological research, using this information to better locate structures and to avoid or lessen water and soil contamination.

Exploration for Energy and Mineral Resources

Over the past century, industries have developed rapidly, populations have grown

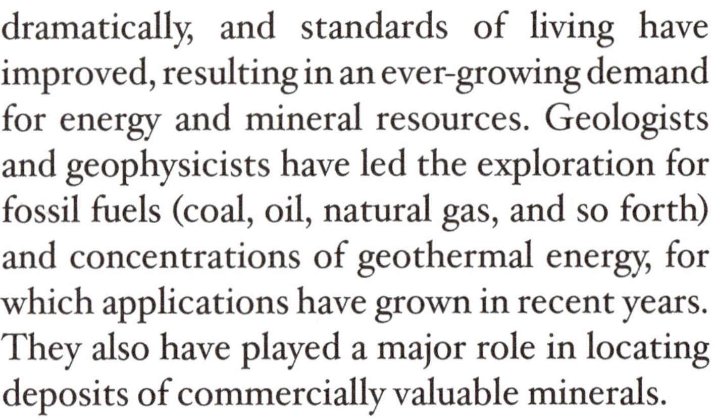

dramatically, and standards of living have improved, resulting in an ever-growing demand for energy and mineral resources. Geologists and geophysicists have led the exploration for fossil fuels (coal, oil, natural gas, and so forth) and concentrations of geothermal energy, for which applications have grown in recent years. They also have played a major role in locating deposits of commercially valuable minerals.

COAL

The Industrial Revolution of the late 18th and 19th centuries was fueled by coal. Though it has been supplanted by oil and natural gas as the primary source of energy in most modern industrial nations, coal nonetheless remains an important fuel.

The US Geological Survey has estimated that only about 2 percent of the world's minable coal has so far been exploited; known reserves should last for at least 300 to 400 years. Moreover, new coal basins continue to be found, as, for example, the lignite basin discovered in the mid-1980s in Rajāsthān in northwestern India.

Coal-exploration geologists have found that coal was formed in two different tectonic

A geologist points to a vein of lignite, a type of coal, that is close to the surface near Amidon, North Dakota. Some geologists search for fossil fuels to help identify sources of energy for the energy industry.

settings: (1) swampy marine deltas on stable continental margins, and (2) swampy freshwater lakes in graben (long, narrow troughs between two parallel normal faults) on continental crust. Knowing this and the types of sedimentary rock formations that commonly include coal, geologists can readily locate coal-bearing areas. Their main concern, therefore, is the quality of the coal and the thickness of the coal bed or seam. Such information can be derived from samples

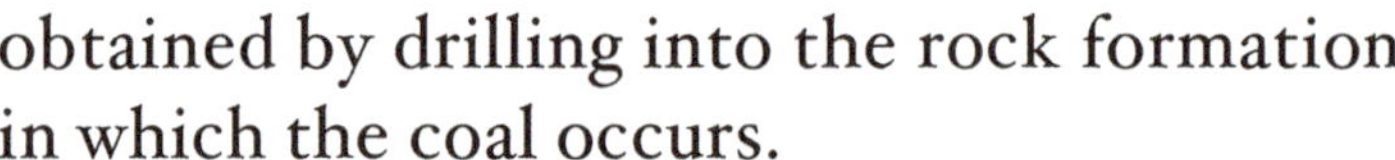

obtained by drilling into the rock formation in which the coal occurs.

Oil and Natural Gas

During the last half of the 20th century, the consumption of petroleum products increased sharply. This led to a depletion of many existing oil fields, notably in the United States, and intensive efforts to find new deposits.

Crude oil and natural gas in commercial quantities are generally found in sedimentary rocks along rifted continental margins and in intracontinental basins. Such environments exhibit the particular combination of geologic conditions and rock types and structures conducive to the formation and accumulation of liquid and gaseous hydrocarbons. They contain suitable source rocks (organically rich sedimentary rocks such as black shale), reservoir rocks (those of high porosity and permeability capable of holding the oil and gas that migrate into them), and overlying impermeable rocks that prevent the further upward movement of the fluids. These so-called cap rocks form petroleum traps.

Petroleum geologists concentrate their search for oil deposits in such geologic

A petroleum geologist surveys a region to map it for possible oil exploration in a desert in Mali.

settings, mapping both the surface and subsurface features of a promising area in great detail. Geologic surface maps show subcropping sedimentary rocks and features associated with structural traps. Maps of this kind may be based on direct observation or may be constructed with photographs taken from aircraft and Earth-orbiting satellites, particularly of terrain in remote areas. Subsurface maps reveal possible hidden underground structures and lateral variations

BOREHOLE SAMPLING

Direct sampling, usually by means of boreholes, is required to make positive identification of ores, fuels, and other materials. It is also necessary for determining their quantity and for selecting methods of recovery. Most deep boreholes are drilled by the rotary method, in which a drill bit is rotated while fluid ("drilling mud") is circulated through the bit to lubricate and cool it and to bring rock chips to the surface where they can be collected and analyzed. Shallow boreholes in hard rock formations are sometimes drilled by a percussion method, whereby a heavy bit is repeatedly raised and dropped to chip away pieces of rock. After a borehole has been drilled, various tools are lowered into the hole to measure different physical properties.

in sedimentary rock bodies that might form a petroleum trap. The presence of such features can be detected by various means, including gravity measurements, seismic methods, and the analysis of borehole samples from exploratory drilling.

Another method used by petroleum geologists in exploratory areas involves the sampling of surface waters from swamps, streams, or lakes. The water samples are analyzed for traces of hydrocarbons, the presence of which would indicate seepage from a subsurface petroleum trap. This geochemical technique, along with seismic profiling, is often used to search for offshore petroleum accumulations.

Once an oil deposit has actually been located and well drilling is under way, petroleum geologists can determine from core samples the depth and thickness of the reservoir rock as well as its porosity and permeability. Such information enables them to estimate the quantity of the oil present and the ease with which it can be recovered.

Although only about 15 percent of the world's oil has been exploited, petroleum geologists estimate that at the present rate of demand the supply of recoverable oil will last no more than 100 years. Because of this rapid depletion of conventional oil sources, economic geologists have explored oil shales and tar sands as potential supplementary petroleum resources. Extracting oil from these substances is, however, very expensive and energy-intensive. In addition, the extraction process (mining and chemical treatment) poses environmental challenges, especially in regions where it occurs. Even so, oil shales and tar sands are abundant, and advances in recovery technology may yet make them attractive alternative energy resources.

El Tatio geyser field is located in the Atacama Desert in Chile. Geologists study geysers for ways to harness geothermal energy for direct-use applications, geothermal heat pumps, and electric power generation, among other uses.

GEOTHERMAL ENERGY

Another alternate energy resource is heat from Earth's interior. The surface expression of this energy is manifested in volcanoes, fumaroles, steam geysers, hot springs, and boiling mud pools. Global heat-flow maps constructed from geophysical data show that the zones of highest heat flow occur along the active plate boundaries. There is, in effect, a close association between geothermal energy sources and volcanically active regions.

A variety of applications have been developed for geothermal energy. For example, public buildings, residential dwellings, and greenhouses in such areas as Reykjavík, Iceland, are heated with water pumped from hot springs and geothermal wells. Hot water from similar sources also is used for heating soil to increase crop production (for example, in Oregon) and for seasoning lumber (as in parts of New Zealand). The most significant application of geothermal energy, however, is the generation of electricity. The first geothermal power station began operation in Larderello, Italy, in the early 1900s. Since then similar facilities have been built in various countries, including Iceland, Japan, Mexico, New Zealand, Turkey, the Tibet Autonomous Region of China, and the United States. In most cases turbines are driven with steam separated from superheated water tapped from underground geothermal reservoirs and geysers.

FUMAROLES

Fumaroles are vents in the Earth's surface from which steam and volcanic gases are emitted. The major source of the water vapor emitted by fumaroles is groundwater heated by bodies of magma lying relatively close to the surface. Carbon dioxide, sulfur dioxide, and hydrogen sulfide are usually emitted directly from the magma. Fumaroles are often present on active volcanoes during periods of relative quiet between eruptions.

Fumaroles are closely related to hot springs and geysers. In areas where the water table rises near the surface, fumaroles can become hot springs. A fumarole rich in sulfur gases is called a solfatara; a fumarole rich in carbon dioxide is called a mofette.

This fumarole is one of many such vents located on Vulcano Island, off northeastern Sicily, in Italy. The fumaroles emit sulfurous vapor that attest to the island's continuous volcanic activity.

MINERAL DEPOSITS

The distribution of commercially significant mineral deposits, the economic factors associated with their recovery, and the estimates of available reserves constitute the basic concerns of economic geologists. Because continued industrial development is heavily dependent on mineral resources, their work is crucial to modern society.

It has long been known that certain periods of Earth history were especially favorable for the concentration of specific types of minerals. Copper, zinc, nickel, and gold are important in Archean rocks; magnetite and hematite are concentrated in early Proterozoic banded-iron formations; and there are economic Proterozoic uranium reserves in conglomerates (a sedimentary rock composed of rounded rock fragments). These mineral deposits and a variety of others that developed throughout the Phanerozoic Eon (about 541 million years ago to the present day) can be related to specific types of plate-tectonic environments. Among the latter are copper, lead, and zinc in intracontinental rifts. An interesting discovery has been the remarkable concentrations of gold, iron, zinc, and copper in brine pools and sulfide-rich muds in the Red Sea and in the Salton Sea in southern California. For example, in many countries copper, nickel, and chromium deposits occur in ophiolite complexes thrust onto the continents from the ocean floor. Tungsten and tin deposits occur in many granites. The correlation of these associations and distributions with periods of Earth history, on the one hand, and plate-tectonic settings, on the other, have enabled regional metallogenetic provinces to

These active "smoker" chimneys precipitate iron, copper, and zinc sulfides in the Mariana Arc region, deep in the Pacific Ocean. Hydrothermal vents form chimneys called black or white smokers when the vents emit mineral particles that build up.

be defined, which have proved helpful in the search for ore deposits.

During the 20th century the exploitation of mineral deposits was so intense that serious depletion of many resources was predicted. Mercury reserves, for example, are particularly low. To deal with this problem, it has become necessary to mine deposits having smaller and smaller workable grades, a trend well illustrated by the copper mining industry, which now extracts copper from rocks with grades as low as 0.2 percent.

Investigators have discovered a major potential metallic source on the deep ocean floor, where there are large concentrations of manganese-rich nodules along with minor amounts of copper, nickel, and cobalt. Such concentrations are especially abundant in three sections of the Pacific Ocean—the area near Hawaii, that northeast of New Zealand, and that west of Central America.

Earthquake Prediction and Control

No natural event is as destructive over so large an area in so short a time as an earthquake.

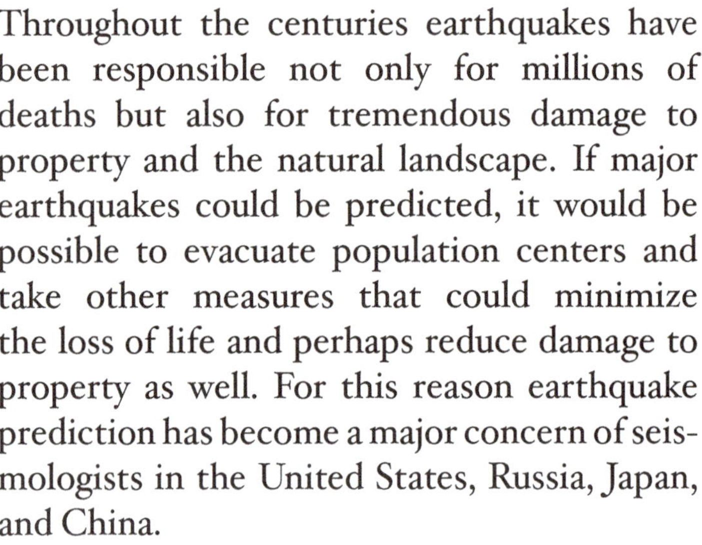

Throughout the centuries earthquakes have been responsible not only for millions of deaths but also for tremendous damage to property and the natural landscape. If major earthquakes could be predicted, it would be possible to evacuate population centers and take other measures that could minimize the loss of life and perhaps reduce damage to property as well. For this reason earthquake prediction has become a major concern of seismologists in the United States, Russia, Japan, and China.

World seismicity patterns show that earthquakes tend to occur along active plate boundaries where there is subduction (Japan) or strike-slip motion (California) and along strike-slip faults (as in China, where they are the result of the northward migration of India into Asia). Investigators agree that much more has to be learned about the physical properties of rocks in fault zones before they are able to make use of changes in these properties to predict earthquakes. The use of the Global Positioning System (GPS) at satellite ground stations over the years is providing quantitative data on a millimeter scale concerning the relative movement of crustal blocks across seismic faults. Recent research has suggested that rocks may become strained shortly before an earthquake and affect such observable properties of the Earth's crust as seismic wave velocity and radon concentration. Leveling surveys and tiltmeter measurements have revealed that deformation in the fault zone just prior to an earthquake may cause changes in ground level and, in certain cases, variations in groundwater level. Some investigators have reported changes in the electric resistivity and remanent magnetization of rocks as precursory phenomena.

Since the San Francisco earthquake of 1906, seismic activity along the nearby San Andreas Fault has been closely monitored. It has been observed that numerous semicontinuous microearthquakes have occurred along some sections of the fault. These small quakes seem to release built-up strain and thus prevent large earthquakes. By contrast, intervening sections of the fault are apparently locked and thus manifest no microshocks. Consequently, seismic strain accumulating in these locked sections is expected to be released one day in a major quake.

Seismological research includes the study of earthquakes caused by human activities, such as impounding water behind high dams,

A seismologist wires a solar power panel to a seismograph in Oklahoma. The seismograph will monitor earthquakes that some believe have been caused by an increase in the number of injection wells used to dispose of waste water from oil and gas drilling.

injecting fluids into deep wells, excavating mines, and detonating underground nuclear explosions. In all of these cases except for deep mining, seismologists have found that the induction mechanism most likely involves the release of elastic strain, just as with earthquakes of tectonic origin. Studies of artificially induced quakes suggest that one possible method of controlling natural earthquakes is to inject fluids into fault zones so as to release strain energy.

Seismologists have done much to explain the characteristics of ground motions recorded in earthquakes. Such information is required to predict ground motions in future earthquakes, thereby enabling engineers to design earthquake-resistant structures. The largest percentage of the deaths and property damage that result from an earthquake is attributable to the collapse of buildings, bridges, and other man-made structures during the violent shaking of the ground. An effective way of reducing the destructiveness of earthquakes, therefore, is to build structures capable of withstanding intense ground motions.

Other Areas of Application

The fields of engineering, environmental, and urban geology are broadly concerned with applying the findings of geologic studies to construction engineering and to problems of land use. The location of a bridge, for example, involves geologic considerations in selecting sites for the supporting piers. The strength of geologic materials such as rock or compacted clay that occur at the sites of the piers should be adequate to support the load placed on

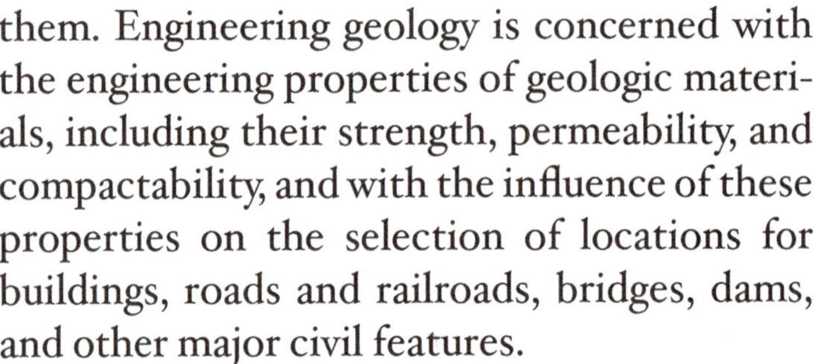

them. Engineering geology is concerned with the engineering properties of geologic materials, including their strength, permeability, and compactability, and with the influence of these properties on the selection of locations for buildings, roads and railroads, bridges, dams, and other major civil features.

Urban geology involves the application of engineering geology and other fields of geology to environmental problems in urban areas. Environmental geology is generally concerned with those aspects of geology that touch on the human environment. Environmental and urban geology deal in large measure with those aspects of geology that directly influence land use. These include the stability of sites for buildings and other civil features, sources of water supply (hydrogeology), contamination of waters by sewage and chemical pollutants, selection of sites for burial of refuse so as to minimize pollution by seepage, and locating the source of geologic building materials, including sand, gravel, and crushed rock. Since the end of the 20th century the importance of environmental geology has increased considerably in most developed countries as societies became aware of the environmental impact of humankind.

CONCLUSION

Modern technological developments have affected all the different geologic disciplines. The impact has been particularly notable in such activities as radiometric dating, experimental petrology, crystallography, chemical analysis of rocks and minerals, micropaleontology, and seismological exploration of Earth's deep interior.

One development in the 21st century has been a debate among geologists and other scholars about whether a new geologic interval, called the Anthropocene, should be created. They have known for decades that humans exerted an enormous pull on Earth's natural resources and have been a significant force in geologic processes. Humans were changing the planet in other ways as well, notably by continuing to influence what happened on Earth's surface, in Earth's atmosphere and oceans, and in biogeochemical nutrient cycling. Incontrovertible evidence of humanity's footprint across the globe first appeared during the "Great Acceleration," a boom period that followed World War II, which was characterized by exponential growth

A geoscientist researches rock samples using a petrographic microscope to study the mineral content of the rocks. Technological developments in equipment and scientific research methods have greatly advanced all disciplines in the field of geology.

in the human population, fossil-fuel use, water use, food production, and international communication and the rapid pace of land-use conversion.

By 2015 humans had modified more than 50 percent of Earth's ice-free land area, having turned much of it into farmland, pastureland, or urban land. The burning of fossil fuels (for example, wood, coal, petroleum, and natural gas) to cook food, provide heat, and generate electrical power, as well as the measures used during the production of concrete for roads and buildings, caused the concentration of carbon dioxide (CO_2) to rise in the atmosphere. (Atmospheric CO_2 had been tracked directly since 1959, when the level stood at 316 parts per million by volume [ppmv]; by 2015 it had risen to 400 ppmv). Rising CO_2 contributed to the increase in Earth's average near-surface air temperature, and climatologists believed that rising temperatures contributed to numerous other changes, including the loss of large amounts of sea ice in the Arctic Ocean and of a number of ice shelves surrounding the Antarctic Peninsula, the reduction in the size of mountain glaciers, and the increased frequency of extreme weather events. Other chemicals, such as lead, sulfur compounds, and chlorofluorocarbons, as well as radioactive isotopes from nuclear testing, also affected the atmosphere and the living things that used it.

Much of the discussion has focused on the advisability of adding a category to the international chronostratigraphic chart, the official chart of the geologic time maintained by the International Commission on Stratigraphy. If the change is made, geologists would also need to decide whether to add the Anthropocene as an epoch (on par with the Holocene Epoch [11,700 years ago to the present]) or as an age within the Holocene. In addition, the interval's starting point would need to be set.

The debate continues. One benefit from the continuing discussion is that it allows people from several walks of life to examine the various impacts humans and their activities have had on the planet, perhaps providing additional opportunities to reevaluate unsustainable lifestyles.

cleavage The quality possessed by a crystallized substance or rock of splitting along definite planes.

deformation The process whereby rocks are folded, faulted, sheared, or compressed by Earth stresses (as in the growth of mountain ranges).

density The quantity of something per unit volume, unit area, or unit length: as the mass of a substance per unit volume.

denudation The action of stripping the covering, or laying bare, as when erosion denudes the rocks of soil.

diagenesis The chemical process by which sediment becomes rock.

diffraction A modification that light undergoes in passing by the edges of opaque bodies or through narrow slits or in being reflected from ruled surfaces, and in which the rays appear to be deflected and produce fringes of parallel light and dark or colored bands.

geoid A model of Earth that coincides with sea level, and serves as a reference from which to gauge topographic heights and ocean depths.

goniometer An instrument for measuring angles (as in surveying or mineralogy).

intrusion The forcible entry of magma into or between other rock formations.

isotope Any of the forms of an element that differ in the number of neutrons in an atom.

lithification The conversion of unconsolidated sediments into solid rock.

luster The appearance of the surface of a mineral with respect to its reflecting qualities.

mass spectrometry An instrumental method for identifying the chemical constitution of a substance by means of the separation of gaseous ions according to their differing mass and charge.

paleomagnetism The intensity and direction of residual magnetism in ancient rocks.

plate tectonics The scientific theory that holds that Earth's lithosphere is divided into a number of plates that float on and travel independently over the mantle, and that much of the Earth's seismic activity occurs at the boundaries of these plates as a result of frictional interaction.

radiogenic isotope An isotope that is produced by a radioisotope's decay and that may or may not be radioactive.

refractive index The ratio of the speed of light in one medium (as air or glass) to that in another medium.

remanent magnetism Also called residual magnetism, magnetization remaining in a magnetized body no longer under external magnetic influence: the magnetism of a permanent magnet.

seismology The science that deals with earthquakes and with artificially produced vibrations of the Earth.

specific gravity The ratio of the density of a substance to the density of some other substance (as water) taken as a standard when both densities are obtained by weighing in air.

spectrometer An analytical instrument used to measure the dispersion of an emission, such as radiation.

strata In geology, a sheetlike mass of sedimentary rock or earth of one kind lying between beds of other kinds.

subduction In plate tectonics, the action or process of the edge of one crustal plate descending below the edge of another.

thermodynamics The area of physics that deals with the mechanical action or relations of heat.

FOR MORE INFORMATION

American Geophysical Union (AGU)
2000 Florida Avenue NW
Washington, DC 20009-1227
(800) 966-2481
Website: http://sites.agu.org
This organization encourages research in Earth and space science.

American Geosciences Institute (AGI)
4220 King Street
Alexandria, VA 22302
(703) 379-2480
Website: http://www.americangeosciences.org
The AGI is a network of organizations that represent geoscientists and offers information to them, and encourages public awareness of the importance of geoscience research and education.

Association for Women Geoscientists (AWG)
12000 North Washington Street, Suite 285
Thornton, CO 80241-3134
(303) 253-9220
Website: http://www.awg.org

The AWG is an international group that works to improve the quality and level of participation of women in the geological sciences.

Canadian Institute of Mining, Metallurgy, and Petroleum (CIM)
Suite 1250, 3500 de Maisonneuve Blvd. W.
Westmount, QC H3Z 3C1
Canada
Tel.: (514) 939-2710
Website: https://www.cim.org
A not-for-profit technical society, the CIM promotes the exchange of research in the field, encourages professional development, and supports the minerals industry.

Geological Association of Canada (GAC)
c/o Department of Earth Sciences
Alexander Murray Building, Room ER4063
Memorial University of Newfoundland
St. John's, NL A1B 3X5
Canada
(709) 864-7660
Website: http://www.gac.ca

The GAC encourages communication among its members and advances the findings in geoscience research and knowledgeable use of the geological sciences by everyone.

National Science Foundation (NSF)
4201 Wilson Boulevard
Arlington, VA 22230
(703) 292-5111
Website: http://www.nsf.gov
An independent federal agency, the NSF funds basic research at U.S. colleges and universities. Its Directorate of Geosciences funds programs in the geological sciences, including atmospheric, Earth, ocean, and polar sciences.

US Geological Survey (USGS)
12201 Sunrise Valley Drive
Reston, VA 20192
(888) 275-8747
Website: http://www.usgs.gov
The USGS, a federal agency, provides scientific information "to describe and understand the Earth." It works to minimize the effects of natural disasters

on people and property and helps to manage natural and mineral resources throughout the United States.

Websites

Because of the changing nature of internet links, Rosen Publishing has developed an online list of websites related to the subject of this book. This site is updated regularly. Please use this link to access the list:

http://www.rosenlinks.com/SCI/geo

FOR FURTHER READING

Anderson, Michael, ed. *Investigating Minerals, Rocks, and Fossils* (Introduction to Earth Science). New York, NY: Britannica Educational Publishing, 2012.

Hollar, Sherman, ed. *Earth and Its Moon* (The Solar System). New York, NY: Britannica Educational Publishing, 2012.

Hollar, Sherman, ed. *Investigating Earth's Desert, Grassland, and Rainforest Biomes* (Introduction to Earth Science). New York, NY: Britannica Educational Publishing, 2012.

Lambert, David. *The Field Guide to Geology*. New York, NY: Facts On File, 2011.

Rafferty, John P., ed. *Geochronology, Dating, and Precambrian Time: The Beginning of the World as We Know It* (The Geologic History of Earth). New York, NY: Britannica Educational Publishing, 2011.

Rafferty, John P., ed. *Glaciers, Sea Ice, and Ice Formation* (Dynamic Earth). New York, NY: Britannica Educational Publishing, 2011.

Rafferty, John P., ed. *Landforms* (Geology: Landforms, Minerals, and Rocks). New York, NY: Britannica Educational Publishing, 2012.

Rafferty, John P., ed. *The Mesozoic Era: Age of Dinosaurs* (The Geologic History of Earth), New York, NY: Britannica Educational Publishing, 2011.

Rafferty, John P., ed. *Minerals* (Geology: Landforms, Minerals, and Rocks). New York, NY: Britannica Educational Publishing, 2012.

Rafferty, John P., ed. *Plate Tectonics, Volcanoes, and Earthquakes* (Dynamic Earth). New York, NY: Britannica Educational Publishing, 2011.

Rafferty, John P., ed. *Rocks* (Geology: Landforms, Minerals, and Rocks). New York, NY: Britannica Educational Publishing, 2012.

INDEX

F

G

H

O

P

R

S